# Foreward

For many of us, this season is a season filled with the hug... and the fireplace, the sound of carols and Mariah Carey's "All I Want For Christmas," and the sight of decorations. While we sing that this is the most wonderful time of the year, the reality for most of us is that it's the *busiest* time of the year! Our senses and our calendars are flooded!

What makes Advent *Advent*, though, is not the flurry of color and caravans, it's not the Christmas parties and Secret Santa exchanges. What makes Advent *Advent* is that it is a season of anticipation. Like Lent, Advent is a season where we are getting ready for something. And something big!

If Lent is the season that prepares us for the Resurrection of our Lord, Advent is the season that prepares us for the Arrival of our Lord. (Hence why we call it Advent: Advent means arrival.) Advent is a season of reflection and repentance. The way that we prepare for Christ's arrival is by preparing ourselves;

personally and communally. We ask in this season, "How can I/we make myself/ourselves ready for the arrival of Jesus?"

This is why we called this resource "Prepare the Way." Quite simply because we are preparing ourselves for the one who called himself the Way! (John 14:6) We hope this resource will be valuable to you as your prepare for Christ's Advent!

What "Prepare the Way" Is

"Prepare the Way" is a devotional, but it is more than a devotional. The foundation of which is a daily reflection. In this sense it is like other devotionals. Unlike other devotionals, though, there are other avenues for Spiritual formation. The various components of "Prepare the Way" are as follows:

Weekly Collect:
The Weekly Collect is a gathering prayer. We hope the Collect will gather your thoughts and center your focus on Christ.

1

Lectio Divina (Sacred Reading):
Each day we read the Scriptures in the promise that the Word of God will read our lives.

Visio Divina (Sacred Vision):
Each week we gaze upon sacred art in the promise that the Word of God will see us.

Audio Divina (Sacred Listening):
Each week we listen to sacred music in the promise that the Word of God hears us.

Camino Divina (Sacred Walking):
Each week we share in a holy practice in the promise that the Word of God walks with us.

Weekly Examen:
The Weekly Examen is a way to look back on the ways that God has been at work in your life and your awareness of it.

We have laid out "Prepare the Way" in such a way that you can easily navigate each resource on each day.

Grace and Peace,
Rev. Danny Quanstrom
Founder, A Plain Account

## Acknowledgments

"Prepare the Way" was made possible through the collaborative efforts of multiple clergy. While we followed the direction of Rev. Jason Buckwalter, no single person is responsible for "Prepare the Way." The A Plain Account team is comprised of practicing clergy; folks who are in the thick of the pastoral office. As such, Prepare the Way is a resource for the church written by people who love the church!

The folks who made "Prepare the Way" possible are Rev. Jason Buckwalter, Rev. Rebecca Dunger Peak, Rev. Alicia McClintic, Rev. Brent Neely, and Rev. Marvin Jones. I would like to thank these folks who do this work simply because they believe in it! There is no one on A Plain Accounts payroll, everyone contributes because they want to resource the church. Without their continued efforts, A Plain Account would not be able the resource that it is!

I am grateful to have such a strong team making A Plain Account the premier Wesleyan resource online. And I am grateful for their excellent work creating "Prepare the Way."

Grace and Peace,
Rev. Danny Quanstrom
Founder, A Plain Account

3

# From the Authors

It is our hope and prayer that you will find *Prepare the Way* to be an important part of your Advent journey. This work is a labor of love for both of us, and simultaneously a means of grace as we meditated on each passage. Rev. Rebecca Dunger Peak wrote the reflections for Monday, Wednesday, and Friday, while Rev. Jason Buckwalter reflected on the passages for Tuesday, Thursday, and Saturday. We have tried to keep the tone light and somewhat informal, while still attending to the spirit of the season and texts. Being the people we are, there are many times we refer to personal experiences and our families. May those stories remind you that the reading and interpreting of scripture is best done amid the nitty-gritty world of families, friends, and church, where tough questions, joys, sorrows, and wonder abound.

Let us prepare the way for the coming of Christ!

Rev. Jason Buckwalter & Rev. Rebecca Dunger Peak

5

# THE FIRST
# WEEK OF
# ADVENT

*Collect*

Almighty God, give us grace to cast away the works of darkness, and put on the armor of light, now in the time of this mortal life in which your Son Jesus Christ came to visit us in great humility; that in the last day, when he shall come again in his glorious majesty to judge both the living and the dead, we may rise to the life immortal; through him who lives and reigns with you and the Holy Spirit, one God, now and forever. Amen.

*Visio Divina* **(Sacred Vision)**

Christ Our Light
(Stained Glass Window in the Holy
Rosary Priory in Bushey, UK)

***Audio Divina*** **(Sacred Listening)**
Songs for Worship
*Come, Thou Long Expected Jesus* - Fernando Ortega
*God with Us* - All Sons & Daughters
CCLI#2113365

Advent Reflection Playlist

***Prayer***
Most High glorious God, enlighten the darkness of my heart. Give me right faith, sure hope and perfect charity. Fill me with understanding and knowledge that I may fulfill your command.
- Saint Francis of Assisi

***Lectio Divina*** **(Sacred Reading)**
Psalm 122, Laetatus sum
I was glad when they said to me,

    "Let us go to the house of the Lord!"
Our feet are standing
    within your gates, O Jerusalem.

Jerusalem—built as a city
    that is bound firmly together.
To it the tribes go up,
    the tribes of the Lord,
      as was decreed for Israel,
      to give thanks to the name of the Lord.
For there the thrones for judgment were set up,
    the thrones of the house of David.

Pray for the peace of Jerusalem:

9

"May they prosper who love you.
Peace be within your walls,
     and security within your towers."
For the sake of my relatives and friends
     I will say, "Peace be within you."
For the sake of the house of the Lord our God,
     I will seek your good.

### *Camino Divina* (Sacred Walking)

Sometime on Sunday, prayerfully light a candle to mark the beginning of your week. We light a candle, in the midst of the darkness of our lives and our world, to symbolize our hopeful longing for Jesus the Messiah; as we do so, may excitement for His coming burn in our hearts.

This week, you may wish to bake something sweet (cookies, cupcakes, brownies, etc.) for someone who might need to experience the hope of Christ. Relax as it bakes in the oven and enjoy the warmth and the sweetness filling your home. Remember that it is sweet to wait and hope in the Lord, and that we are called to share hope with others.

*Lectio Divina (Sacred Reading)*

**Psalm 124**

If it had not been the Lord who was on our side
—let Israel now say—
if it had not been the Lord who was on our side,
when our enemies attacked us,
 then they have swallowed us up alive,
when their anger was kindled against us;
then the flood would have swept us away,
the torrent would have gone over us;
then over us would have gone
the raging waters.
Blessed be the Lord,
who has not given us
as prey to their teeth.
We have escaped like a bird
from the snare of the fowlers;
the snare is broken,
and we have escaped.
Our help is in the name of the Lord,
who made heaven and earth.

*Additional Texts: Genesis 8:1-19; Romans 6:1-11*

**The Conditional Clause**

There's nothing quite like a conditional clause to inspire action. My Mom's favorite conditional clause goes something like this: If you don't eat your peas, you won't get dessert. You might think I would be inspired to eat said vegetable. Instead, I was inspired to skip dessert. Fortunately for us, the conditional clauses prevalent in today's readings are much more hope-full.

11

The song of ascents of Psalm 124 was very likely a communal song intoned by the Israelites as they went up to the temple in Jerusalem for three festivals: Passover, Pentecost, and Sukkot, or the Feast of Booths. As the song leader bellowed the beginning of the conditional clause, "If it had not been the LORD who was on our side—let Israel now say—" the pilgrims would have immediately chimed in with the retelling of God's deliverance punctuating every "then" as if it were the downbeat of the measure. Every stanza becomes a cause for thanksgiving—every glimmer of a story inspiring their journey. Every verse builds its rhythm to the crescendo of a blessing: "Blessed be the Lord, who has not given us as prey to their teeth. We have escaped...and we have escaped." The song finds its resolution in an affirmation of faith, a renewed understanding of the very unchanging nature of God: "Our help is in the name of the LORD, who made heaven and earth." Not only would the rehearsal of God's deliverance be motivation for the journey, but it would inspire a life of faithfulness to the God who is faithful. The song stirred up the spark of hope within the pilgrims.

Paul stirs up that spark of hope within the Roman Christ-followers by taking them back to the beginning of their life of faith when all was made new in the waters of their baptism. The flood story in Genesis is a powerful reminder of God's habit of redeeming creation and now, people, through the gift of water to wipe away the stain of sin. Being baptized into Christ means being welcomed into the fullness of his life, including his death and resurrection. It may seem an odd juxtaposition to wrap our minds around being baptized into Jesus 'death at a time of year in which we are preparing for his coming and coming again. If baptism is that wonderful convergence of a three-fold grace, where they meet, marry, and move us forward into newness of life, then Paul targets justifying grace aligned with Jesus 'work on the cross. Yet the Apostle's conditional statement in verse 5, his crescendo, reminds us that death never has the last word.: "For if we have been united with [Jesus] in a death like his, we will certainly be united with him in a resurrection like his." Read that verse again; this time, substitute "since" for "if." That simple translation change magnifies and intensifies its hope-full message that leads to a glorious resolution (v. 11): So you also must, in this present moment, consider yourselves dead to sin and alive to God in Christ Jesus. Paul's certainty erases any doubt. May these truths be music to your ears.

*Prayer: Oh God, we confess that our hope rests in your coming and your coming again. Grant us the strength to rest in you. Amen.*

*Lectio Divina (Sacred Reading)*

**Hebrews 11:32-40**

And what more should I say? For time would fail me to tell of Gideon, Barak, Samson, Jephthah, of David and Samuel and the prophets— who through faith conquered kingdoms, administered justice, obtained promises, shut the mouths of lions, quenched raging fire, escaped the edge of the sword, won strength out of weakness, became mighty in war, put foreign armies to flight. Women received their dead by resurrection. Others were tortured, refusing to accept release, in order to obtain a better resurrection. Others suffered mocking and flogging, and even chains and imprisonment. They were stoned to death, they were sawn in two, they were killed by the sword; they went about in skins of sheep and goats, destitute, persecuted, tormented — of whom the world was not worthy. They wandered in deserts and mountains, and in caves and holes in the ground.

Yet all these, though they were commended for their faith, did not receive what was promised, since God had provided something better so that they would not, apart from us, be made perfect.

**Delayed Gratification**

I remember hearing of an experiment testing delayed gratification in children. The experiment was simple, cookies or marshmallows were placed before a child, and they were given a choice. The child could have the treat now, or if they waited until later, they could have two treats. The self-control it took to delay the gratification of eating a treat would be rewarded with more goodies. Some kids in the experiment ate the treat right away, while others did not. Patience and discipline are important parts of human character. Some naturally have an overabundance of those traits; others do not. Some learn to develop patience and discipline, and others were never taught how.

14

While today's passage isn't about delayed gratification, the author of Hebrews does point out that patience and discipline are important elements of faith and hope. One of the more famous passages in Scripture, Hebrews chapter 11, narrates a timeline of faithful characters in God's redemption story. After spending a considerable amount of space telling us about Abraham and Moses, the author of Hebrews plows through the rest of Israel's history rather quickly.

We get the sense that the author of Hebrews believes that the characters who exhibit faithful patience and discipline are legion. If there were enough time and writing material, the author would tell the tails of all those who followed God faithfully. This last section of chapter 11 has a twist; many fail to see the outcome of their hope and faith. It was as if someone sat down Gideon and Jephthah, placing a cookie in front of them with the promise that if they didn't eat the cookie now but went out and lived obedient lives, one day they would receive two cookies. But all of those the author mentions died before they could receive their reward for patience and disciplined hope. What's worse, some of the faithful remained so despite torture and persecution.

The next chapter starts with an admonition for the author's readers to exercise their hope-filled patience and discipline, regardless of what treatment they might endure, before seeing their hope fulfilled. The admonition is as relevant for us as it was for those who first read Hebrews. Only, I'm afraid that the church has too often sugar-coated what comes with a life of following Jesus. Somehow, we've come to believe that as followers of Jesus, we can eat our cookies now *and* later. We want the good feeling of following Jesus without wanting the consequences of following Jesus. We want the manger, but not the cross, Christmas but not Good Friday.

If anything, the author of Hebrews wants us to understand that even when the world is at its worst, when all seems lost, when we suffer on account of our insistence that power is made perfect in weakness and in the power of suffering love, that our hope in God's work in the world will not be disappointed. So, as we prepare the way for Jesus 'coming as a baby in a manger, let us hold fast to the hope that all things will be made new.

Prayer: *Oh God, we confess we are weak, impatient, and lack discipline. Grant us the strength to work and live in the hope that your work of restoration and redemption will one day be completed. Amen.*

THE FIRST WEEK OF ADVENT

# WEDNESDAY

*Lectio Divina (Sacred Reading)*

**Isaiah 54:1-10**

Sing, O barren one who did not bear;
 burst into song and shout,
 you who have not been in labor!
For the children of the desolate woman will be more
 than the children of her that is married, says the Lord.
Enlarge the site of your tent,
 and let the curtains of your habitations be stretched out;
 do not hold back; lengthen your cords
 and strengthen your stakes.
For you will spread out to the right and to the left,
 and your descendants will possess the nations
 and will settle the desolate towns.

Do not fear, for you will not be ashamed;
 do not be discouraged, for you will not suffer disgrace;
 for you will forget the shame of your youth,
 and the disgrace of your widowhood you will remember no more.
For your Maker is your husband,
 the Lord of hosts is his name;
 the Holy One of Israel is your Redeemer,
 the God of the whole earth he is called.
For the Lord has called you
 like a wife forsaken and grieved in spirit,
 like the wife of a man's youth when she is cast off,
 says your God.
For a brief moment I abandoned you,
 but with great compassion I will gather you.
In overflowing wrath for a moment

17

I hid my face from you,
but with everlasting love I will have compassion on you,
says the Lord, your Redeemer.

This is like the days of Noah to me:
Just as I swore that the waters of Noah
would never again go over the earth,
so I have sworn that I will not be angry with you
and will not rebuke you.
For the mountains may depart
and the hills be removed,
but my steadfast love shall not depart from you,
and my covenant of peace shall not be removed,
says the Lord, who has compassion on you.

*Additional Texts: Psalm 124; Matthew 24:23-35*

### Coffee With Jesus

At one time, a thought-provoking four-panel comic, Coffee with Jesus, was a regular feature of my Facebook newsfeed. In any of the comics, we find one of five characters in conversation with Jesus about any number of concerns or issues of the day. Sometimes the reader bears witness to humor. Other times, challenge. And still others, mercy. This modernized rendering of a coffee-sipping Jesus is present in the fullness of life.

Today Isaiah invites us to bear witness to a similar conversation with God and Israel, the barren one who has borne no children, the desolate woman. It is helpful to remember the prophet was the intermediary between God and Israel during their exile in Babylon. From the very start of the chapter, there are commands for joy in the midst of desolation: shout for joy, burst into song, enlarge the site of your tent, stretch out your curtains, lengthen your cords, strengthen your stakes. These are commands laden with hope and certainty that Israel will once again come home. God encourages them to prepare the way for a time of increase, a time of renewal.

At once hopeful, this holy conversation feels intimate. These conversations require a level of vulnerability among the conversation partners. Israel is present in the shame of behaviors that lead to their destruction, discouragement, and disgrace. Sociologist Brené Brown reminds us that shame shapes our identity.

While guilt would have the Israelites say they did something bad, shame would have them say they are bad. Yet God, equally vulnerable in this conversation, reveals parts of God's identity: I am your Maker, the LORD of hosts, the Holy One of Israel, your Redeemer. This is the One who removes their fear and shame, replacing them with the promise of a new day dawning.

This intimate, holy conversation provides the space for God, in a very human way, to process both actions and emotions. The hint is the use of "but" in verses 7 through 10. Pay attention to your everyday conversations. When you or your conversation partner use the word "but," it is a subtle and often unintentional way of negating everything spoken before it. Pay extra attention to what follows "but." In God's case, a brief abandonment is followed by a future gathering. A gathering that will be done with great compassion, not just plain old compassion or even mediocre compassion. The qualifier "great" is a tip-off to how good this gathering will be. A moment of overflowing wrath and hiding God's face is followed by a future compassion motivated by everlasting love. This is a portrait of redemption from the mouth of their Redeemer. These future tense promises are sealed with an oath: "I will not be angry with you and will not rebuke you" (v9). This oath is God renewing God's side of the covenant before any renewal of a commitment by Israel. God intends this to be a binding covenant: "my steadfast love shall not depart from you, and my covenant of peace shall not be removed" (v10). No matter what else may be removed from the Israelites by others, no outside force will ever be able to remove God's steadfast love and covenant of peace. Oh, how grace sneaks up on us! Do you hear echoes of Paul's words to the Romans: "For I am convinced that neither death, nor life, nor angels, nor rulers, nor things present, nor things to come, nor powers, nor height, nor depth, nor anything else in all creation will be able to separate us from the love of God in Christ Jesus our Lord" (Rom. 8:38-39, NRSVUE).

*Prayer: Oh God, thank you for your great compassion, your steadfast love, and your faithfulness. We confess our hope that your coming will bring everlasting peace. Amen.*

*Lectio Divina (Sacred Reading)*

**Psalm 72**

Give the king your justice, O God,
    and your righteousness to a king's son.
May he judge your people with righteousness,
    and your poor with justice.
May the mountains yield prosperity for the people,
    and the hills, in righteousness.
May he defend the cause of the poor of the people,
    give deliverance to the needy,
    and crush the oppressor.

May he live while the sun endures,
    and as long as the moon, throughout all generations.
May he be like rain that falls on the mown grass,
    like showers that water the earth.
In his days may righteousness flourish
    and peace abound, until the moon is no more.

May he have dominion from sea to sea,
    and from the River to the ends of the earth.
May his foes bow down before him,
    and his enemies lick the dust.
May the kings of Tarshish and of the isles
    render him tribute,
  may the kings of Sheba and Seba
    bring gifts.
May all kings fall down before him,
    all nations give him service.

For he delivers the needy when they call,

the poor and those who have no helper.
He has pity on the weak and the needy,
and saves the lives of the needy.
From oppression and violence he redeems their life;
and precious is their blood in his sight.

Long may he live!
May gold of Sheba be given to him.
May prayer be made for him continually,
and blessings invoked for him all day long.
May there be abundance of grain in the land;
may it wave on the tops of the mountains;
may its fruit be like Lebanon;
and may people blossom in the cities
like the grass of the field.
May his name endure forever,
his fame continue as long as the sun.
May all nations be blessed in him;
may they pronounce him happy.

Blessed be the Lord, the God of Israel,
who alone does wondrous things.
Blessed be his glorious name forever;
may his glory fill the whole earth.
Amen and Amen.

**Prayers for the King**
These days, it may seem hard to pray for our elected leaders. That is, of course, if they aren't of the same political persuasion we are. Maybe we do pray for them, but the prayer calls for their political downfall and not a prayer for a lavish blessing of wisdom, justice, and mercy. Politics have always been messy, but things might seem more chaotic now than they used to be. We're just so divided.

Our divisions make it hard for us to pray Psalm 72 in the same way as Israel might have. To be sure, our situation is vastly different than Israel's. We're not a theocratic monarchy, after all. Still, Psalm 72 oozes with positive intersessions on behalf of the King. I find it interesting that the plea made in verse is about justice. Justice is the first quality Israel hopes its King can possess in abundance.

That's followed by righteousness, which in the Old Testament is almost always connected with justice. Both terms are relational in nature. Justice seeks fairness, redemption, and restoration; justice seeks the lifting up of the oppressed. Righteousness seeks friendship.

As the psalm moves on, Israel prays for the King to have a long life of ruling over the world. And gold, too. All too often, when we seek to participate in God's mission in the world, we pray for gold first. We don't really pray for gold, but we do often believe that if only we had enough resources, we could transform God's good world. The psalmist's intent is clear; justice and righteousness come before material support. Perhaps we should pray for God to help us (and our leaders!) to have justice and righteousness without seeking the resources to make our programs run well. Would we make a greater impact in the world by doing so?

Israel prayed this prayer when things were going well, but I imagine that as time went on, the nation split into two, and as they were carried off into exile, they began to pray a little differently. Did Israel begin to pray this psalm with hopeful expectation for the arrival of the Messiah, the King of Kings and Lord of Lords?

Even if Israel did not read this psalm messianically, we should. We should pray Psalm 72 because our world is divided and broken. We should pray this psalm because our leaders often make a mess of the places they have been elected to rule. We should pray Psalm 72 because we desperately need a Messiah who will lead us with justice and righteousness. We need a Messiah to whom all nations will bow down. We need a Messiah who delivers the needy and the poor, who has pity on the weak, who redeems the lives of the oppressed from violence.

Thankfully, that Messiah has come and is coming again, and Jesus is his name. We read and pray this psalm during advent because we believe that our hopeful anticipations for a Messiah have been and are being fulfilled in the birth of Jesus in a manger. He is coming with justice. He is coming with righteousness. He is coming to deliver, redeem, and restore. As we hopefully wait for Christmas, may we pray that we have the strength to follow in his just and right footsteps.

*Prayer: Oh God, we hopefully await your coming in justice and righteousness. Please help us to learn to follow in your footsteps. Amen.*

*Lectio Divina (Sacred Reading)*

**Isaiah 30:19-26**

Therefore the Lord waits to be gracious to you;
> therefore he will rise up to show mercy to you.

For the Lord is a God of justice;
> blessed are all those who wait for him.

Truly, O people in Zion, inhabitants of Jerusalem, you shall weep no more. He will surely be gracious to you at the sound of your cry; when he hears it, he will answer you. Though the Lord may give you the bread of adversity and the water of affliction, yet your Teacher will not hide himself any more, but your eyes shall see your Teacher. And when you turn to the right or when you turn to the left, your ears shall hear a word behind you, saying, "This is the way; walk in it." Then you will defile your silver-covered idols and your gold-plated images. You will scatter them like filthy rags; you will say to them, "Away with you!"

He will give rain for the seed with which you sow the ground, and grain, the produce of the ground, which will be rich and plenteous. On that day your cattle will graze in broad pastures; and the oxen and donkeys that till the ground will eat silage, which has been winnowed with shovel and fork. On every lofty mountain and every high hill there will be brooks running with water—on a day of the great slaughter, when the towers fall. Moreover the light of the moon will be like the light of the sun, and the light of the sun will be sevenfold, like the light of seven days, on the day when the Lord binds up the injuries of his people, and heals the wounds inflicted by his blow.

*Additional Texts Psalm 72:1-7, 18-19; Acts 13:16-25*

**Larger than Life**

In all of scripture, there are these larger-than-life people we relate to at one time or another along our journey of faith—the matriarchs and patriarchs, judges and

24

kings, prophets and poets, disciples and apostles. I once had a dream so vivid that I immediately connected to Joseph, the dreamer, and interpreter of dreams. In my dream, God's disembodied voice instructed me to embark on a journey, the destination of which was unknown to me. I was to journey with a particular companion, pack only a bag with necessary provisions, a map, a compass, and a full gas tank. We would know where we were to go by listening to God's voice at every turn. This dream was a call from God to a ministry of being sent, to go where God needed me, relying on God's provisions. In a sense, our journey through Advent is a "sent" journey. Along the way, we are guided by the voice of God, who speaks to us through scripture with a particular destination: the advent of Christ. Isaiah writes, "…when you turn to the right or when you turn to the left, your ears shall hear a word behind you, saying, 'This is the way; walk in it.'" (Isaiah 30:21, NRSVUE)

This was King David's prayer for Solomon, a prayer intoned in today's Psalm. David sings to God of his dreams for his son's leadership as a king of God's people: equip him. He prayed that God would give Solomon the gift of discernment so that he may judge well with righteousness and justice, using a moral compass that seeks the benefit of the poor, oppressed, and needy. The fruits of such a reign include prosperity, flourishing righteousness, and abundant peace. We can almost see David nudging his son's side as he whispers in his ear, "This is my prayer for you. This is the way; walk in it."

The prophet, writing through a post-exilic lens, names the experience of the Israelites. "You have known war, the desolation of home, suffering at the hands of your captors, the plight of an alien in a foreign land, and our gracious God hears your cries. Not only does God hear, but God also answers." Isaiah points to a God who saves, a God who shows up—on purpose. The answer is tinged with the grace of a gracious God. The human response then is to recognize that the images and practices that accompany those idols they've embraced in a foreign land must be shed, destroyed as if they are unclean. This act of repentance has a far-reaching impact. This turn-around ushers in the transformation of both humanity and all of creation. This great act of salvation, of binding injuries and healing wounds, will be ushered in by a great light by day and by night, a light that pierces the darkness and illuminates the way that we might walk in it.

Hundreds of years later, the Apostle Paul rehearses salvation history in a word of encouragement that serves as a postscript to the reading of the laws and prophets in the synagogue service. He charts a map like a cartographer, pinpointing God's saving work from the exodus to the conquest to the kings, namely David, to Jesus. The prophet had promised the Israelites, "your Teacher will not hide himself any longer, but your eyes shall see your Teacher" (Is. 30:20, NRSVUE). Paul's message of hope shone a light on the Teacher, Jesus. This was his way of nudging his congregation in their sides, whispering in their ears, "This is the way; walk in it."

*Prayer: Oh God, we confess that we routinely fail to remember your past mighty acts of salvation. As we hope for your coming, help us walk in the direction we should go.*

*Lectio Divina (Sacred Reading)*

**Isaiah 40:1-11**

Comfort, O comfort my people,
        says your God.
Speak tenderly to Jerusalem,
        and cry to her
    that she has served her term,
        that her penalty is paid,
    that she has received from the Lord's hand
        double for all her sins.

A voice cries out:
    "In the wilderness prepare the way of the Lord,
        make straight in the desert a highway for our God.
Every valley shall be lifted up,
        and every mountain and hill be made low;
    the uneven ground shall become level,
        and the rough places a plain.
Then the glory of the Lord shall be revealed,
        and all people shall see it together,
        for the mouth of the Lord has spoken."

A voice says, "Cry out!"
        And I said, "What shall I cry?"
    All people are grass,
        their constancy is like the flower of the field.
The grass withers, the flower fades,
        when the breath of the Lord blows upon it;
        surely the people are grass.
The grass withers, the flower fades;
        but the word of our God will stand forever.

27

Get you up to a high mountain,
    O Zion, herald of good tidings;
lift up your voice with strength,
    O Jerusalem, herald of good tidings,
    lift it up, do not fear;
say to the cities of Judah,
    "Here is your God!"
See, the Lord God comes with might,
    and his arm rules for him;
his reward is with him,
    and his recompense before him.
He will feed his flock like a shepherd;
    he will gather the lambs in his arms,
and carry them in his bosom,
    and gently lead the mother sheep.

**Frail and Fleeting**

Isaiah 40 is one of the most recognizable scriptures read during the season of Advent. The words are familiar, and the imagery is iconic. Isaiah's words are as relevant for us today as they were for Israel as the nation longed for God's salvation to come and set the world to rights. Every time I read a passage like this I am stricken by the reminder that the coming of the Messiah is always participatory. We're called to enter into God's work in our world.

What can't be missed, however, is the reminder that what Israel needed saving from was their own destructive choices. While Isaiah's words are tender and full of comfort, Israel is reminded that the penalty for their sins has been paid. They have served their time, but the work is not yet done. A voice cries out for Israel to prepare the way for God's coming salvation. Israel is to blaze a straight path through the wilderness. The path will be smooth and level, making travel on that path as easy as possible.

The picture of Israel's participation in preparing for God's coming contrasts with a reminder that human lives are frail and fleeting. We're like grass that withers on a hot day. We're like a flower that blooms but only for a short time. The contrast between the call to participate in the preparations for God's coming and the reminder that we are frail and fleeting reminds us that our participation in God's work is contingent upon God's generous gift of strength.

As the passage continues, the anticipation of God's arrival is fulfilled. Hope has been fulfilled. God comes with the fullness of God's power to rule, yes, but also to shepherd. Again, we have contrasting images. God is proclaimed mighty to rule, yet gentle and maternal as little lambs are embraced while mother sheep are led to safety.

Like Israel, we must be reminded that the suffering we undergo is often a result of our destructive choices. We must also be reminded that the penalty for our sins has been paid. At the same time, we are called into God's mission in the world. We are called to prepare the way for the Messiah, the one who comes in strength to rule yet who is tender and loving as well. As we participate in God's mission, in preparing the way for God's Kingdom to come in its fullness, we will be tempted to believe that we can make the path straight on our own. As much as we need to be reminded of who God is and what God is doing, we must also be reminded that we are frail and fleeting. Our ability to prepare the way for God's work is only as good as our faith that God will give us the strength and wisdom to do so.

*Prayer: Oh God, thank you for coming to save us. Grant us the strength to prepare the way for your arrival.*

**The Examen**
*Ask God for Illumination*

Speak to us O Lord.
Speak to us as wait and as we watch,
Speak to us as we hope and as we long,
As we sorrow, sigh, and rejoice.
Speak to us throughout these days of Advent
As we await the coming of Christ our King
And stay by us Lord we pray
Until you come again.

*Give Thanks*
- What can you give thanks for from this week?
- Remember the ways God has sustained and carried you this week

*Review the Week*
- Where have I seen God this week?

- Look at this past week through the eyes of God, rather than my own

*Name your Shortcomings*
- Reflect on those areas where you did not love God and neighbor as you should
- Reflect on those things left undone that should be done, and those things done that should not have been done

*Ask for forgiveness*
- Embrace this Upcoming Week
- Ask God where you need to be this week
- Ask God where you might meet God and neighbors this week

# THE SECOND WEEK OF ADVENT

*Collect*

Merciful God, who sent your messengers the prophets to preach repentance and prepare the way for our salvation: Give us grace to heed their warnings and forsake our sins, that we may greet with joy the coming of Jesus Christ our Redeemer; who lives and reigns with you and the Holy Spirit, one God, now and forever. Amen.

*Visio Divina* **(Sacred Vision)**

Peaceable Kingdom by John August
Swanson

***Audio Divina*** **(Sacred Listening)**
Songs for Worship
*Even So, Come* - Chris Tomlin
*Here Comes Heaven* - Elevation Worship
CCLI#2113365

Advent Reflection Playlist

***Prayer***
O Lord Jesus Christ, you are the sun of the world, evermore arising, and never
going down, which by your most welcome appearing and sight, brings forth,
preserves, nourishes, and refreshes all things, as well that are in heaven as also
that are on earth;

We beg you mercifully and faithfully to shine in our hearts, so that the night and
darkness of sins, and the mist of errors on every side may be driven away; with
you brightly shining in our hearts we may all our life go without stumbling or
offense, and may decently and seemly walk as in the day time, being pure and
clean from the works of darkness, and abounding in all good works which God
has prepared us to walk in; you who with the Father and with the Holy Ghost
live and reign for ever and ever. Amen.
- Thomas Cranmer


***Lectio Divina*** **(Sacred Reading)**
Psalm 72:1-7, 18-19 - Deus, judicium
Give the king your justice, O God,
        and your righteousness to a king's son.
May he judge your people with righteousness,
        and your poor with justice.
May the mountains yield prosperity for the people,

33

and the hills, in righteousness.
May he defend the cause of the poor of the people,
   give deliverance to the needy,
   and crush the oppressor.

May he live while the sun endures,
   and as long as the moon, throughout all generations.
May he be like rain that falls on the mown grass,
   like showers that water the earth.
In his days may righteousness flourish
   and peace abound, until the moon is no more.

Blessed be the Lord, the God of Israel,
   who alone does wondrous things.
Blessed be his glorious name forever;
   may his glory fill the whole earth.
   Amen and Amen.


*Camino Divina* **(Sacred Walking)**
Sometime on Sunday, prayerfully light a candle to mark the beginning of your week. We light a candle as an act of repentance, recognizing our sin and our need for a Savior, but also remembering that in Christ we are forgiven and free.

This week, you may wish to prepare a special meal for your household, with as many courses as you can think of. Think about and pray for the people who will share the meal while you are preparing, setting the table with the good stuff, and getting ready to sit down together. As you prepare for dinner, remember what it means to prepare the way of the Lord and to anticipate his arrival with expectancy and joy.

*Lectio Divina (Sacred Reading)*

**1 Thessalonians 4:1-12**

Finally, brothers and sisters, we ask and urge you in the Lord Jesus that, as you learned from us how you ought to live and to please God (as, in fact, you are doing), you should do so more and more. For you know what instructions we gave you through the Lord Jesus. For this is the will of God, your sanctification: that you abstain from fornication; that each one of you know how to control your own body in holiness and honor, not with lustful passion, like the Gentiles who do not know God; that no one wrong or exploit a brother or sister in this matter, because the Lord is an avenger in all these things, just as we have already told you beforehand and solemnly warned you. For God did not call us to impurity but in holiness. Therefore, whoever rejects this rejects not human authority but God, who also gives his Holy Spirit to you.

Now concerning love of the brothers and sisters, you do not need to have anyone write to you, for you yourselves have been taught by God to love one another; and indeed, you do love all the brothers and sisters throughout Macedonia. But we urge you, beloved, to do so more and more, to aspire to live quietly, to mind your own affairs, and to work with your hands, as we directed you, so that you may behave properly toward outsiders and be dependent on no one.

*Additional Texts:Psalm 21; Isaiah 24:1-16a; 1 Thessalonians 4:1-12*

**Fruit of the Sanctified**

Among Paul's many gifts is his ability to speak truth in the cultural context of his congregation. We who live thousands of years later miss out on the nuances. The Christ follower in Thessalonica lived in a port city along the Aegean Sea. On an active trade route, this brought the world to their door. It just so happened to be the capital city of the Roman province of Macedonia. Scholar Edgar M. Krentz notes that while they were devoted to the imperial cult of Rome ...

culturally it remained a Greek city governed by Greek law."* Paul's audience were converts who did not have a Jewish background. The surrounding culture was steeped in the philosophical schools of Stoicism and Epicureanism. The former focused on a life grounded in ethics that makes the adherent more virtuous and brings a state of happiness accompanied by a sense of peace. The latter was a school of philosophy and a form of hedonism that sought the absence of both pain and fear and the growth of tranquility through the pursuit of pleasure.

Paul uses the language and posture of philosophy to remind his congregation that, just as their Gentile counterparts live a life guided by ethics, as a people set apart by God through sanctification, they, too, live according to an ethic shaped by a covenant relationship with both God and neighbor. The Holy Spirit, a gift directly from the heart of God, fuels their desire and ability to live a sanctified life from the moment they choose to become a Christ follower. Paul wasn't opposed to sexual pleasure within a covenant relationship. In fact, sexual intimacy within a covenant relationship was especially encouraged on the Sabbath as a way to strengthen the bonds between the covenant partners. Paul was, however, opposed to sexual relations that caused harm and led to the exploitation of another person since each person is created in the image of God.

The Apostle shifts the conversation to another kind of love. The Greek word to describe this love of the brothers and sisters, *philadelphia*, is only used only one other time by Paul in his letter to the Romans. Paul calls to mind the great commandments of loving God and neighbor, for when we love our neighbor in word and deed, we demonstrate our love of God. The two are inextricably linked. As he urges them to love their siblings in Christ throughout Macedonia "more and more," he encourages them to act in ways that will stir up that spark of grace, trusting that God will give them more. God's grace is not only sufficient, it is abundant.

Paul is explicit about the dichotomies of a life lived under the authority of God versus human authority for a reason. There is a sense of urgency to his argument because he believes the return of Christ is imminent in his own lifetime. He wants these Christ-followers in Thessalonica to be prepared. His greatest desire is that their lives bear the fruit of a sanctified, holy life that not only seeks the welfare of other people but of all creation. Through God's gift of the Spirit, we are free, as John Wesley said, to do all the good we can, by all the means we can, in all the ways we can, in all the places we can, at all the times we can, to all the people we can, as long as ever we can.

*Prayer: Oh God, as we prepare for your coming, help us to bear the fruit of a holy and sanctified life, always seeking the good of the other.*

* Meeks, Wayne A., General Editor. The HarperCollins Study Bible, New Revised Standard Version, with the Apocryphal/Deuterocanonical Books (New York: HarperCollins Publishers, 1993) 2218-19.

*Lectio Divina (Sacred Reading)*

**1 Thessalonians 5:12-28**

But we appeal to you, brothers and sisters, to respect those who labor among you, and have charge of you in the Lord and admonish you; esteem them very highly in love because of their work. Be at peace among yourselves. And we urge you, beloved, to admonish the idlers, encourage the fainthearted, help the weak, be patient with all of them. See that none of you repays evil for evil, but always seek to do good to one another and to all. Rejoice always, pray without ceasing, give thanks in all circumstances; for this is the will of God in Christ Jesus for you. Do not quench the Spirit. Do not despise the words of prophets, but test everything; hold fast to what is good; abstain from every form of evil.

May the God of peace himself sanctify you entirely; and may your spirit and soul and body be kept sound and blameless at the coming of our Lord Jesus Christ. The one who calls you is faithful, and he will do this.

Beloved, pray for us. Greet all the brothers and sisters with a holy kiss. I solemnly command you by the Lord that this letter be read to all of them. The grace of our Lord Jesus Christ be with you.

**In all Circumstances**

"Encourage the fainthearted, help the weak." "Always seek to do good to one another and to all." "Rejoice always, pray without ceasing, give thanks in all circumstances." "Don't quench the Spirit." Paul offers his final thoughts to the church in Thessalonica, and the result is like trying to drink water from a fire hose. Paul packs so much advice in these short verses it is hard to find a focal point. It's as if Paul was about to run out of paper, but he had so much more to say, so he condensed it down to its present form.

As we read this passage in the season of Advent, I wonder how following Paul's admonitions might help prepare us for Jesus 'birth and subsequent life and ministry. If we live the way Paul hopes, will we be better prepared to accept the kind of Messiah Jesus came to be? I believe we will.

If we learn to be at peace among ourselves, we will have an easier time accepting that Jesus came not to condemn the world, not to antagonize it, but to save the world. If we encourage the fainthearted and help the weak, being patient with those who cannot help themselves, we'll be better able to recognize just how patient Jesus has been with us when we are weak and unable to help ourselves.

When we refuse to repay evil with evil, we'll understand that violence is not the way of the Kingdom of God.

When we choose to give thanks in all circumstances, we'll be able to focus on the sacrificial nature of the Christian life. What we see when we truly look at Jesus is that faithfulness often leads to suffering. We will see that faithfulness is always about doing good to everyone.

If we take the time to listen and contemplate the prophetic speech our pastors offer, we open ourselves up to seeing the world through the eyes of Jesus. If we let it, the prophetic word reshapes our imagination, helping us to see past the way the world is now toward a realization of the Kingdom of God.

While the list Paul gives us is difficult, I believe it's possible for us to live with peace, patience, and joy. Verses 23-24 bring it all together. "May the God of peace himself sanctify you entirely; and may your spirit and soul and body be kept sound and blameless at the coming of our Lord Jesus Christ. The one who calls you is faithful, and he will do this." We can live faithful lives, not on our own power, but only when we give ourselves over to the sanctifying power of God's Spirit. We can be prepared and help prepare the way for Jesus 'arrival because the one who calls us into relationship is faithful.

*Prayer: Oh God, help us to give ourselves over to your sanctifying power so that we might be prepared for your coming. Grant us the strength to live with peace, patience, and joy in all circumstances so that we might prepare the way for your coming.*

# WEDNESDAY

*Lectio Divina (Sacred Reading)*

**Genesis 15:1-21**

After these things the word of the Lord came to Abram in a vision, "Do not be afraid, Abram, I am your shield; your reward shall be very great." But Abram said, "O Lord God, what will you give me, for I continue childless, and the heir of my house is Eliezer of Damascus?" And Abram said, "You have given me no offspring, and so a slave born in my house is to be my heir." But the word of the Lord came to him, "This man shall not be your heir; no one but your very own issue shall be your heir." He brought him outside and said, "Look toward heaven and count the stars, if you are able to count them." Then he said to him, "So shall your descendants be." And he believed the Lord; and the Lord reckoned it to him as righteousness.

Then he said to him, "I am the Lord who brought you from Ur of the Chaldeans, to give you this land to possess." But he said, "O Lord God, how am I to know that I shall possess it?" He said to him, "Bring me a heifer three years old, a female goat three years old, a ram three years old, a turtledove, and a young pigeon." He brought him all these and cut them in two, laying each half over against the other; but he did not cut the birds in two. And when birds of prey came down on the carcasses, Abram drove them away.

As the sun was going down, a deep sleep fell upon Abram, and a deep and terrifying darkness descended upon him. Then the Lord said to Abram, "Know this for certain, that your offspring shall be aliens in a land that is not theirs, and shall be slaves there, and they shall be oppressed for four hundred years; but I will bring judgment on the nation that they serve, and afterward they shall come out with great possessions. As for yourself, you shall go to your ancestors in peace; you shall be buried in a good old age. And they shall come back here in the fourth generation; for the iniquity of the Amorites is not yet complete."

When the sun had gone down and it was dark, a smoking fire pot and a flaming torch passed between these pieces. On that day the Lord made a covenant with Abram, saying, "To your descendants I give this land, from the river of Egypt to the great river, the river Euphrates, the land of the Kenites, the Kenizzites, the Kadmonites, the Hittites, the Perizzites, the Rephaim, the Amorites, the Canaanites, the Girgashites, and the Jebusites."

*Additional Texts: Psalm 21; Matthew 12:33-37*

**How Long?**
How long is too long to hold onto a promise? How long before doubt creeps in? The answer for Abram is three chapters. Way back in Genesis 12, when God made the promise of land, offspring, and blessing, Abram was 75 years old. Yes, Abram wanted someone to carry on the family business and inherit the estate. I suspect he also longed to sit around the fire with his heirs sharing the stories of faith that prompted their journey, stories of God's redeeming work, tales of abundance and deliverance. Like all of us, he wanted to leave a legacy that pointed to God's faithfulness.

By chapter 15, Abram needs to be reassured that God's promises haven't expired. Perhaps the doubt that creeps in is laced with fear—fear that he is no longer worthy to receive the promises fulfilled. Perhaps he is too old and Sarai too infertile, he wonders. There's no indication that Abram called out to God in the midst of his doubts about both offspring and land. Rather the LORD simply shows up during the turmoil that surfaces in doubt's wake. With each doubt, the LORD renews the promise with exponential proportions. Abram's descendants will be more numerous than the stars in the heavens. I imagine Abram's jaw went slack with awe in response. His wordless expression a sign of renewed belief which the LORD interpreted as righteousness.

This righteousness prompted the LORD'S renewed promise of the land. Yet preparations were necessary for the next portion. Thus, Abram became an active participant in bringing together all the pieces for the ritual sacrifice and preventing scavenging animals from defiling it. He gladly invested his resources, time, and energy in eager anticipation. His active participation in the preparations transformed his doubts and fears into hope. While this covenant-making ritual is foreign to post-modern ears, it was commonly practiced in Mesopotamia and noted in Jeremiah 34:17-22. Jon D. Levenson describes the ritual as a self-curse: "Those walking between the pieces will be like the dead animals if they violate the covenant. In the case at hand, remarkably, it is the LORD, symbolized by the 'smoking [fire pot] 'and 'flaming torch '(15:17), who invokes the self-curse, and nothing is said about any covenantal obligations that Abram is to fulfill."* Abram was active in making preparations for the covenant that became the foundation of the promise that came with a caveat clothed in a prophecy: Abram's descendants would be oppressed and enslaved for four centuries, but God will deliver them to the promised land with all they would need to survive and thrive. Even though his descendants would suffer for a time, Abram would live long and prosper and finally come to rest in peace alongside his ancestors. Simply put, the caveat: the fulfillment of promises requires patience. Abram's peaceful rest would be a direct result of his trust in the LORD'S redeeming work and a promise sealed in a covenant. Abram awaited the advent of a promise fulfilled, even if it would be realized beyond his lifetime.

In this holy season, we await the promise of God in the coming of Christ. Like Abram, may our active participation in the preparations of this season transform our doubts and fears into hope. May we invest our resources, time, and energy in eager anticipation. May we wait with a patience that gives rise to peace. May we rejoice in this covenant renewal with our Redeeming God.

*Prayer: Oh God, as we await your coming, help us to rest in the promise of your salvation, even when their fulfillment is long in coming.*

*Berlin, Adele and Brettler, Marc Zvi, eds. The Jewish Study Bible: Jewish Publication Society Tanakh Translation. (New York: Oxford University Press, 2004) 35-36.

*Lectio Divina (Sacred Reading)*

**Psalm 37**

Do not fret because of the wicked;
> do not be envious of wrongdoers,
for they will soon fade like the grass,
> and wither like the green herb.

Trust in the Lord, and do good;
> so you will live in the land, and enjoy security.
Take delight in the Lord,
> and he will give you the desires of your heart.

Commit your way to the Lord;
> trust in him, and he will act.
He will make your vindication shine like the light,
> and the justice of your cause like the noonday.

Be still before the Lord, and wait patiently for him;
> do not fret over those who prosper in their way,
> over those who carry out evil devices.

Refrain from anger, and forsake wrath.
> Do not fret—it leads only to evil.
For the wicked shall be cut off,
> but those who wait for the Lord shall inherit the land.

Yet a little while, and the wicked will be no more;
> though you look diligently for their place, they will not be there.
But the meek shall inherit the land,
> and delight themselves in abundant prosperity.

The wicked plot against the righteous,

and gnash their teeth at them;
but the Lord laughs at the wicked,
 for he sees that their day is coming.

The wicked draw the sword and bend their bows
 to bring down the poor and needy,
 to kill those who walk uprightly;
their sword shall enter their own heart,
 and their bows shall be broken.

Better is a little that the righteous person has
 than the abundance of many wicked.
For the arms of the wicked shall be broken,
 but the Lord upholds the righteous.

The Lord knows the days of the blameless,
 and their heritage will abide forever;
they are not put to shame in evil times,
 in the days of famine they have abundance.

But the wicked perish,
 and the enemies of the Lord are like the glory of the pastures;
 they vanish—like smoke they vanish away.

The wicked borrow, and do not pay back,
 but the righteous are generous and keep giving;
for those blessed by the Lord shall inherit the land,
 but those cursed by him shall be cut off.

Our steps are made firm by the Lord,
 when he delights in our way;
though we stumble, we shall not fall headlong,
 for the Lord holds us by the hand.

I have been young, and now am old,
 yet I have not seen the righteous forsaken
 or their children begging bread.
They are ever giving liberally and lending,
 and their children become a blessing.

Depart from evil, and do good;

so you shall abide forever.
For the Lord loves justice;
he will not forsake his faithful ones.

The righteous shall be kept safe forever,
but the children of the wicked shall be cut off.
The righteous shall inherit the land,
and live in it forever.

The mouths of the righteous utter wisdom,
and their tongues speak justice.
The law of their God is in their hearts;
their steps do not slip.

The wicked watch for the righteous,
and seek to kill them.
The Lord will not abandon them to their power,
or let them be condemned when they are brought to trial.

Wait for the Lord, and keep to his way,
and he will exalt you to inherit the land;
you will look on the destruction of the wicked.

I have seen the wicked oppressing,
and towering like a cedar of Lebanon.
Again I passed by, and they were no more;
though I sought them, they could not be found.

Mark the blameless, and behold the upright,
for there is posterity for the peaceable.
But transgressors shall be altogether destroyed;
the posterity of the wicked shall be cut off.

The salvation of the righteous is from the Lord;
he is their refuge in the time of trouble.
The Lord helps them and rescues them;
he rescues them from the wicked, and saves them,
because they take refuge in him.

**Waiting Patiently**

By nature, I am not a very patient person. With home improvement projects, cooking, or some other activity where I must follow directions to achieve the desired result, I have a hard time following the steps in the order or time required to do them. I often think, "This should be done by now! Forty-seven more steps! I bet I can get done in thirty-five!" Or, with projects where I've got to do some research to gain the proper knowledge or skill to complete, I have a tendency to skip or skim the required reading just so I can get on with the project. Regardless of the project, home improvement, cooking, or some other thing, when I don't patiently wait through the instructions or the proper time to let something boil or dry, the end is usually a disaster!

I think, if we are honest with ourselves, this is often our approach to Christianity and understanding or living as citizens in God's Kingdom. We don't want to wait. Sometimes, the instructions seem stupid. Or worse, impractical. In our impatience to see the world changed or our lives changed, we skip steps or skim the required reading and think to ourselves, "I'm smart. I can figure this out by myself!"

Worse yet, maybe we consult others who seem smarter than us who offer us books or web pages with titles like, "Seven Simple Steps to [insert whatever you'd like]" or "Easy Ways to Have Your Best Life!" Now, there may be some nuggets of truth and goodness contained in offerings like those, but they give into our base attitude of impatience. Like home improvement projects, life is never as simple and straightforward as it seems on the cover. This is equally true for the Christian life. While the idea of Christianity, that Jesus died and was raised again for our sins, granting us the power to live like him through the power of his Holy Spirit, might seem like a simple enough idea, practically living it out isn't. And that's without folks around us who are constantly acting in evil ways.

The Psalmist reminds us, though, that the goal is not to reach the finish line first. The goal is to wait "Be still before the Lord, wait patiently for him...." It may seem like the wicked prosper and that God is taking his good old sweet time to do anything about it but worrying and fretting will only get you in trouble. No, waiting patiently is the key. God will not often solve our problems, evil people, our own self-imposed deficiencies, or whatever, instantly. We must wait. But waiting isn't passive; it's an active working that means we follow God's instructions. We read the directions, not skipping some of them because they seem inconsequential or impractical.

We may not be very patient people, but God calls us to do the hard work of waiting, not rushing ahead but waiting, learning, and trusting that God is going to work something good out of every situation.

*Prayer: Oh God, grant us the ability to wait patiently for you. Help us to sit, listen, read, pray, and learn about you and how you would have us live in this world. Amen.*

*Lectio Divina (Sacred Reading)*

**2 Peter 3:11-18**
Since all these things are to be dissolved in this way, what sort of persons ought you to be in leading lives of holiness and godliness, waiting for and hastening the coming of the day of God, because of which the heavens will be set ablaze and dissolved, and the elements will melt with fire? But, in accordance with his promise, we wait for new heavens and a new earth, where righteousness is at home.

Therefore, beloved, while you are waiting for these things, strive to be found by him at peace, without spot or blemish; and regard the patience of our Lord as salvation. So also our beloved brother Paul wrote to you according to the wisdom given him, speaking of this as he does in all his letters. There are some things in them hard to understand, which the ignorant and unstable twist to their own destruction, as they do the other scriptures. You therefore, beloved, since you are forewarned, beware that you are not carried away with the error of the lawless and lose your own stability. But grow in the grace and knowledge of our Lord and Savior Jesus Christ. To him be the glory both now and to the day of eternity. Amen.

*Additional Texts: Psalm 146:5-10; Ruth 4:13-17*

*Hesed*
The first generation of Christ followers were abuzz with hope! They had every expectation that Jesus would return in their lifetime. They were certain they would experience the sights, sounds, and smells of the new heavens and a new earth. And why not? The apostles wrote of it in their letters and spoke of it in synagogues and amphitheaters. The excitement of something new and the hope of an end to the hardships of the day were motivations for following The Way.

49

Yet the more time passed without the expected renewal of all creation; the more people sought answers and direction, the more they fought discouragement. As the apostles and disciples realized Jesus might not return in their lifetime, their teaching shifted. There is an assurance in Peter's second letter that the promise is still alive. There is yet cause for hope. And here are some suggestions while you wait. In truth, these suggestions carry more weight than mere "shoulds." These are "oughts," commands without wiggle room: strive, regard, beware, and grow. Strive to be pure, without fault. This ensures that when Jesus finds you, you won't feel guilty, but you will be at peace. Regard the delay in the Lord's return as the gift of time to share your faith and lead others to repentance, conversion, and salvation. When we are discouraged, we are prone to temptation in thought and action. So, beware that you don't get carried away. Instead, grow in grace and knowledge of our Lord and Savior, Jesus Christ. Peter could have written, "Tend to works of piety and works of mercy to prevent backsliding."

Peter was nothing if not practical in his advice on how best to prepare for the time of waiting. His command to grow in knowledge as we wait for the coming of Christ points to God's Word as a tool for motivation. The Psalm of the day provides ample motivation by reminding us of the character and nature of the One for whom we wait: the creator and ever-faithful redeemer. This is the very LORD whose actions are not confined to one time and place. This is the One who

- frees exiles,
- opens eyes,
- lifts up the lowly,
- loves the righteous,
- watches over and upholds the strangers, orphans, and widows, those who lack the protection of a human family or tribe.

Lest there be any doubt, the Lord will reign forever!

If that weren't motivation enough, the passage from Ruth shows how God, working in the background, watched over and upheld the foreigner, Ruth, and the widow, Naomi. The two women and Boaz are living examples of God's great *hesed* (Hebrew for God's steadfast love and faithfulness) for God's people. They demonstrate extravagant love, care, grace, compassion, and mercy for others. This great *hesed* isn't simply a matter of faith; it's in their DNA as evidenced by the fruit of their faith, a DNA that works its way through the family tree from Ruth and Boaz to Obed, to Jesse, to David, and all the way to Jesus, the One for whom we prepare as we wait in this holy season.

*Prayer: Oh God, as we wait for your coming, help us grow in the grace and knowledge of the Lord.*

*Lectio Divina (Sacred Reading)*

## Luke 3:1-18

In the fifteenth year of the reign of Emperor Tiberius, when Pontius Pilate was governor of Judea, and Herod was ruler of Galilee, and his brother Philip ruler of the region of Ituraea and Trachonitis, and Lysanias ruler of Abilene, during the high priesthood of Annas and Caiaphas, the word of God came to John son of Zechariah in the wilderness. He went into all the region around the Jordan, proclaiming a baptism of repentance for the forgiveness of sins, as it is written in the book of the words of the prophet Isaiah,

"The voice of one crying out in the wilderness:
'Prepare the way of the Lord,
make his paths straight.
Every valley shall be filled,
and every mountain and hill shall be made low,
and the crooked shall be made straight,
and the rough ways made smooth;
and all flesh shall see the salvation of God. " '

John said to the crowds that came out to be baptized by him, "You brood of vipers! Who warned you to flee from the wrath to come? Bear fruits worthy of repentance. Do not begin to say to yourselves, 'We have Abraham as our ancestor'; for I tell you, God is able from these stones to raise up children to Abraham. Even now the ax is lying at the root of the trees; every tree therefore that does not bear good fruit is cut down and thrown into the fire."

And the crowds asked him, "What then should we do?" In reply he said to them, "Whoever has two coats must share with anyone who has none; and whoever has food must do likewise." Even tax collectors came to be baptized, and they asked him, "Teacher, what should we do?" He said to them, "Collect no more than the amount prescribed for you." Soldiers also asked him, "And we, what should we do?" He said to them, "Do not extort money from anyone by threats or false accusation, and be satisfied with your wages."

As the people were filled with expectation, and all were questioning in their hearts concerning John, whether he might be the Messiah, John answered all of them by saying, "I baptize you with water; but one who is more powerful than I is coming; I am not worthy to untie the thong of his sandals. He will baptize you with the Holy Spirit and fire. His winnowing fork is in his hand, to clear his threshing floor and to gather the wheat into his granary; but the chaff he will burn with unquenchable fire."

So, with many other exhortations, he proclaimed the good news to the people.

**Grant us Strength**
Today's passage is filled with vivid imagery, imagery that calls us to prepare the way for the coming of the Messiah. I'm afraid, however, that we often fail to recognize how the flow of the passage connects preparing for the coming of the Messiah with repentance, bearing good fruit, and baptism with the Holy Spirit. This time of year, it is too easy to get caught up in the hopeful expectation of the salvation Jesus brings that we miss how we are to prepare the way for his arrival.

That John is meant to prepare Israel for Jesus 'coming is a given. With images taken straight from Israel's prophets, Luke reminds us that we have a part to play in preparing the world for Jesus 'coming. In the church, we often understand the preparation we're to do has to do with telling others about the good news Jesus brings. That's not wrong, but it's only half the story.

Read in the context of Luke's gospel, John's message is directed at people who should have already been prepared for the coming of the Messiah. The language John uses is strong, calling Israel's faithful a "brood of vipers!" A warning is given along with a call to bear good fruit. In this instance, Israel cannot rest on their heritage. No, they need to repent and begin bearing good fruit, or they'll get chopped down as any dead tree deserves. Preparing the way for the Messiah begins with Israel's repentance. Preparing the way for the Messiah begins with the Church's repentance. Of what might we need to repent today?

For their part, the crows understand the gist of what John is encouraging them to do, even if they fail to know how exactly to do it. John instructs them toward living lives characterized by justice and righteousness. The two examples John

53

gives have to do with being intentional about not exploiting others for personal gain. Preparing the way for the Messiah begins with a fair amount of self-reflection to see if we are living with justice and righteousness toward our neighbors.

Finally, John admits that the baptism he offers is a lead-in to the baptism which the Messiah will bring. What the water begins, the Holy Spirit will finish. The image of what baptism with the Spirit looks like is appropriate. When Jesus comes bringing the Spirit with him, the extraneous and unusable elements will be burnt away. The chaff will vanish as wisps of smoke. We might be tempted to read John's words as judgmental. And, in a sense, they are. The Spirit judges that which is extraneous and unusable to the work of God in our world and burns it away leaving us in a continued state of refreshed cleanliness. Preparing the way for the coming of the Messiah begins with the removal of things within us that inhibit God's good news from doing its work around us. Israel has much that needed to be burned away. What in us, and not just personally but corporately, might need to be burnt away so that God's good news can do its work in, though, and around us? Come Holy Spirit, burn out our chaff with unquenchable fire!

*Prayer: Oh God, thank you for inviting us into preparing the way for your coming and your coming again. Strengthen us so we might have the courage to repent, to live with justice and righteousness. Help us to sit still long enough to have our chaff burnt away. Amen.*

**The Examen**
*Ask God for Illumination*

Speak to us O Lord.
Speak to us as wait and as we watch,
Speak to us as we hope and as we long,
As we sorrow, sigh, and rejoice.
Speak to us throughout these days of Advent
As we await the coming of Christ our King
And stay by us Lord we pray
Until you come again.

*Give Thanks*
- What can you give thanks for from this week?

- Remember the ways God has sustained and carried you this week

*Review the Week*
- Where have I seen God this week?
- Look at this past week through the eyes of God, rather than my own

*Name your Shortcomings*
- Reflect on those areas where you did not love God and neighbor as you should
- Reflect on those things left undone that should be done, and those things done that should not have been done

*Ask for forgiveness*
- Embrace this Upcoming Week
- Ask God where you need to be this week

# THE THIRD WEEK OF ADVENT

*Collect*

Stir up your power, O Lord, and with great might come among us; and, because we are sorely hindered by our sins, let your bountiful grace and mercy speedily help and deliver us; through Jesus Christ our Lord, to whom, with you and the Holy Spirit, be honor and glory, now and forever. Amen

*Visio Divina* (**Sacred Vision**)

Mary's Song by Lauren Wright Pittman

***Audio Divina* (Sacred Listening)**
Songs for Worship
*What A Beautiful Name* - Hillsong Worship
*O Come, O Come Emmanuel* - For King & Country
CCLI#2113365

Advent Reflection Playlist

***Prayer***
O merciful God, fill our hearts, we pray you, with the graces of your Holy Spirit, with love, joy, peace, long-suffering, gentleness, goodness, faith, meekness, temperance. Teach us to love those who hate us, to pray for those who despitefully use us, that we may be the children of you our Father, who makes your sun to shine on the evil and on the good and sends rain on the just and on the unjust. In adversity grant us grace to be patient; in prosperity keep us humble; may we guard the door of our lips; may we lightly esteem the pleasures of this world, and thirst after heavenly things; through Jesus Christ our Lord. Amen.
- Saint Anselm

***Lectio Divina* (Sacred Reading)**
Psalm 146:4-9 - Lauda, anima mea
When their breath departs, they return to the earth;
    on that very day their plans perish.

Happy are those whose help is the God of Jacob,
    whose hope is in the Lord their God,
who made heaven and earth,
    the sea, and all that is in them;
    who keeps faith forever;
who executes justice for the oppressed;
    who gives food to the hungry.

    The Lord sets the prisoners free;
the Lord opens the eyes of the blind.

The Lord lifts up those who are bowed down;
the Lord loves the righteous.
The Lord watches over the strangers;
he upholds the orphan and the widow,
but the way of the wicked he brings to ruin.


*Camino Divina* (**Sacred Walking**)

Sometime on Sunday, prayerfully light a candle to mark the beginning of your week. We light a candle in celebration of God's restoration—past and yet to come—knowing we can rejoice because the Lord is near.

This week you may wish to watch a funny movie, and to sync up with long distance family or friends. Call each other and press play at the same time, so you're able to be together-while-apart. Be sure it's a "laugh-out-loud" sort of movie and laugh loudly together. Enjoy the gift of JOY together. Remember that we have received good news of great joy.

*Lectio Divina (Sacred Reading)*

**Psalm 42**

As a deer longs for flowing streams,
  so my soul longs for you, O God.
My soul thirsts for God,
  for the living God.
When shall I come and behold
  the face of God?
My tears have been my food
  day and night,
while people say to me continually,
  "Where is your God?"

These things I remember,
  as I pour out my soul:
how I went with the throng,
  and led them in procession to the house of God,
with glad shouts and songs of thanksgiving,
  a multitude keeping festival.
Why are you cast down, O my soul,
  and why are you disquieted within me?
Hope in God; for I shall again praise him,
  my help and my God.

My soul is cast down within me;
  therefore I remember you
from the land of Jordan and of Hermon,
  from Mount Mizar.
Deep calls to deep
  at the thunder of your cataracts;
all your waves and your billows

have gone over me.
By day the Lord commands his steadfast love,
    and at night his song is with me,
    a prayer to the God of my life.

I say to God, my rock,
    "Why have you forgotten me?
    Why must I walk about mournfully
        because the enemy oppresses me?"
As with a deadly wound in my body,
    my adversaries taunt me,
    while they say to me continually,
    "Where is your God?"

Why are you cast down, O my soul,
    and why are you disquieted within me?
    Hope in God; for I shall again praise him,
    my help and my God.

*Additional Texts: Isaiah 29:17-24; Acts 5:12-16*

**Thirsting for Something Deeper**
There's something about the night, the darkness, the quiet, that opens space in our minds and hearts to ponder the mysteries of life. This was my experience the year I served as a chaplain resident at two hospitals in Houston, Texas. Whenever we were on-call, we spent the night in the hospital with two beepers, one for the adult hospital and the other for the children's hospital. There were nights when the beepers would chirp non-stop, calling me from one emergency to another. I sat with patients and their families. I coordinated care with staff. And when it was quiet and still, and the beepers were silent, I might even make my way to one of my assigned units to check in on any particular needs. More often than not, both patients and staff were in a deep sense of wonder.

I discovered that when everything slows, as it often does at night, people are willing to be more vulnerable, laying down the masks they wear by day. Perhaps the word "CHAPLAIN" embroidered in capital letters on my lab coat provided a sense of safety to even the non-religious or other-religious folks. They would open up as they surveyed the landscape of their life in that particular moment. In their voices, I could hear a longing, a thirsting for something deeper. I could hear the question undergirding it all, "Why are you cast down, O my soul, and why are you disquieted within me?" Time and again, during our conversations, I would reach for the small Bible in my pocket; mind you, this was in the days before cell phones and Bible apps. These folks were looking for meaning, healing, answers, and hope. They were in a place of distress, and the waiting for answers and healing seemed to stir the waters of anxiety that roiled and boiled. As I slowly and calmly read Psalm 42, I could hear an audible release of breath. These beloved children of our Creator heard an ancient psalmist speak the truth of their own souls: they longed for a reason to hope, to rejoice. The Psalmist utilizes the gift of memory to move from despair to joy. The act of remembering and sharing our story allows us to make sense of our journey. As we participate in this ritual of remembering and sense-making, we discover the fingerprints of grace in moments when God's presence was seemingly imperceptible. Suddenly there is a recognition:

> By day the Lord commands his steadfast love,
> and at night his song is with me,
> a prayer to the God of my life.

In the moment of recognition, there is a visible and audible release. Then a lightness of being. Then a deep sense of peace that pervades and surpasses all understanding. It's there that we discover the glowing seeds of resilience. Like the Psalmist, we, too, can have a soul that's simultaneously cast down and disquieted and actively hoping in God, trusting that we will one day rejoice again. Oh, the sacred paradox!

As we enter into this third week of waiting, we might just discover we need the permission this Psalm extends to both breathe and allow the sacred paradox to exist in our own souls. In these darkening days of Advent, may you know there is reason to rejoice.

*Prayer: Oh God, help us to always rejoice in the memories of your past acts of salvation.*

*Lectio Divina (Sacred Reading)*

### Jude 1:17-25

But you, beloved, must remember the predictions of the apostles of our Lord Jesus Christ; for they said to you, "In the last time there will be scoffers, indulging their own ungodly lusts." It is these worldly people, devoid of the Spirit, who are causing divisions. But you, beloved, build yourselves up on your most holy faith; pray in the Holy Spirit; keep yourselves in the love of God; look forward to the mercy of our Lord Jesus Christ that leads to eternal life. And have mercy on some who are wavering; save others by snatching them out of the fire; and have mercy on still others with fear, hating even the tunic defiled by their bodies.

Now to him who is able to keep you from falling, and to make you stand without blemish in the presence of his glory with rejoicing, to the only God our Savior, through Jesus Christ our Lord, be glory, majesty, power, and authority, before all time and now and forever. Amen.

### Focus!

It's confession time. Almost every time someone says something like we find in Jude, "In the last time there will be scoffers, indulging their own ungodly lusts," as a way to prove that we're living at the end of days, I roll my eyes just a bit. I mean no disrespect to Jude, the Apostle's he quotes, or the good saints who insist we're living close to the end times, it's just that there have always been scoffers who indulge in their ungodly lusts.

Part of the problem is that what follows statements like these in Scripture often gets ignored. All too often, we focus on the moral depravity inherent in our world without focusing on the hope that comes with the advent of Jesus Christ. Jude's words beginning in verses 20-21 are just as important as the reminder that there will always be those who refuse the love that God desires to give. "But you, beloved, build yourselves up on your most holy faith; pray in the Holy Spirit; keep yourselves in the love of God; look forward to the mercy of our Lord Jesus Christ that leads to eternal life."

Jude calls us to focus on the work God is doing in us through the work of the Spirit rather than the corruption around us. Rather than give into the fear constantly shouted around us, we are to keep ourselves in the love of God. That doesn't mean seclusion, though. It's a reminder that what God has surrounded us with is stronger than sin or the death it produces. While fearing death is natural, the love of God gives us the hope that death will never be our ultimate end. Jude gives a nod to the very real threat to life and limb by encouraging us to focus on the mercy which we have and will continue to receive, mercy that leads to eternal life.

My eldest son is fond of reminding us that shenanigans beget shenanigans. The same can be said for fear, and it's equally true for mercy. Mercy begets mercy. The love and mercy we have received from God were never intended to stop with us, regardless of the chaotic state of the world around us. Jude makes this clear, "And have mercy on some who are wavering; save others by snatching them out of the fire; have mercy on still others with fear, hating even the tunic defiled by their bodies." While I'm not entirely sure what to make of the last part of verse 23, Jude's point is clear. As the fear, scoffing, and moral depravity of the world around us increases, so must the nature of our merciful responses increase.

May Jude's benediction serve as our corporate prayer for each other,

*Prayer: Now to him who is able to keep you from falling, and to make you stand without blemish in the presence of his glory with rejoicing, to the only God our Savior, through Jesus Christ our Lord, be glory, majesty, power, and authority, before all time and now and forever. Amen.*

*Lectio Divina (Sacred Reading)*

**Zechariah 8:1-17**

The word of the Lord of hosts came to me, saying: Thus says the Lord of hosts: I am jealous for Zion with great jealousy, and I am jealous for her with great wrath. Thus says the Lord: I will return to Zion, and will dwell in the midst of Jerusalem; Jerusalem shall be called the faithful city, and the mountain of the Lord of hosts shall be called the holy mountain. Thus says the Lord of hosts: Old men and old women shall again sit in the streets of Jerusalem, each with staff in hand because of their great age. And the streets of the city shall be full of boys and girls playing in its streets. Thus says the Lord of hosts: Even though it seems impossible to the remnant of this people in these days, should it also seem impossible to me, says the Lord of hosts? Thus says the Lord of hosts: I will save my people from the east country and from the west country; and I will bring them to live in Jerusalem. They shall be my people and I will be their God, in faithfulness and in righteousness.

Thus says the Lord of hosts: Let your hands be strong—you that have recently been hearing these words from the mouths of the prophets who were present when the foundation was laid for the rebuilding of the temple, the house of the Lord of hosts. For before those days there were no wages for people or for animals, nor was there any safety from the foe for those who went out or came in, and I set them all against one other. But now I will not deal with the remnant of this people as in the former days, says the Lord of hosts. For there shall be a sowing of peace; the vine shall yield its fruit, the ground shall give its produce, and the skies shall give their dew; and I will cause the remnant of this people to possess all these things. Just as you have been a cursing among the nations, O house of Judah and house of Israel, so I will save you and you shall be a blessing. Do not be afraid, but let your hands be strong.

65

For thus says the Lord of hosts: Just as I purposed to bring disaster upon you, when your ancestors provoked me to wrath, and I did not relent, says the Lord of hosts, so again I have purposed in these days to do good to Jerusalem and to the house of Judah; do not be afraid. These are the things that you shall do: Speak the truth to one another, render in your gates judgments that are true and make for peace, do not devise evil in your hearts against one another, and love no false oath; for all these are things that I hate, says the Lord.

*Additional Texts: Psalm 42; Matthew 8:14-17, 28-34*

**The Cutting Table**
During my senior year of high school, I had the joy of working at a regional fabric and craft store. I was a "specialist" at the cutting table. Artists would pile their bolts of fabric on the table, and I would measure and cut the required amount like an expert. At the end of each shift, I gathered up the bolts of fabric. If a bolt had less than one yard of material, the fabric was measured, folded, tagged, and added to a bin of remnants. They were the leftovers. There wasn't enough of any one fabric to make much of anything. It was a sad bin that rarely attracted attention except for a coworker who had a knack for creating the most amazing fiber art from the most eclectic fabrics. Her eyes lit up as she combed through her "treasure" bin. Her enthusiasm was captivating! With a little prodding, she would share her vision. I could almost see it coming to life. The operative word is almost. The challenge for visionary people is to energize others with a glimpse of the future that's so captivating it inspires action.

Through the prophet Zechariah, God does just that. God's zeal for this vision of transforming the remnant of Jerusalem into a faithful, fruitful, holy city filled with old folk, really old folk, and a bountiful number of children playing in the streets is indeed energizing. These weren't just the leftovers of Jerusalem and Judah. God delighted in them as treasures. Yet for that remnant for whom exile was a very present reality, this vision may have appeared too good to be true. So God offers a challenge, "Even though it seems impossible to the remnant of this people in these days, should it also seem impossible to me?" (Zech. 8:6, NRSVUE) This vision is a renewal of an intentional relationship between God and God's people that is rooted in faithfulness and righteousness. As One who saves, delivers, protects, and provides in abundance, God lays out a vision for the future that is cause for rejoicing. This vision is so very different from their current reality. It is one of restoration. Lest this vision be overwhelming, God admonishes both Jerusalem and Judah not once but repeatedly, "Do not be afraid, but let your hands be strong." They would need strong hands and fearless hearts for the work God charged them with in preparation for the realization of the vision: "speak truth to one another, render in your gates judgments that are true and make for peace, do not devise evil in your hearts against one another and love no false oath" (Zech. 8:16-17, NRSVUE). The vision not only restores the relationship between God and all of Israel but also the relationship between the people. In this way, we become co-workers with God in realizing this vision. What could be more powerful than intentionally seeking reconciliation with others as a way of preparing for the advent of Jesus? In this, I am sure God will rejoice.

*Prayer: Oh God, forgive us the times when we fail to see your vision for creation. Help us to be unafraid as you strengthen our weak hands.*

*Lectio Divina (Sacred Reading)*

**2 Samuel 7:1-17**

Now when the king was settled in his house, and the Lord had given him rest from all his enemies around him, the king said to the prophet Nathan, "See now, I am living in a house of cedar, but the ark of God stays in a tent." Nathan said to the king, "Go, do all that you have in mind; for the Lord is with you."

But that same night the word of the Lord came to Nathan: Go and tell my servant David: Thus says the Lord: Are you the one to build me a house to live in? I have not lived in a house since the day I brought up the people of Israel from Egypt to this day, but I have been moving about in a tent and a tabernacle. Wherever I have moved about among all the people of Israel, did I ever speak a word with any of the tribal leaders of Israel, whom I commanded to shepherd my people Israel, saying, "Why have you not built me a house of cedar?" Now therefore thus you shall say to my servant David: Thus says the Lord of hosts: I took you from the pasture, from following the sheep to be prince over my people Israel; and I have been with you wherever you went, and have cut off all your enemies from before you; and I will make for you a great name, like the name of the great ones of the earth. And I will appoint a place for my people Israel and will plant them, so that they may live in their own place, and be disturbed no more; and evildoers shall afflict them no more, as formerly, from the time that I appointed judges over my people Israel; and I will give you rest from all your enemies. Moreover, the Lord declares to you that the Lord will make you a house. When your days are fulfilled and you lie down with your ancestors, I will raise up your offspring after you, who shall come forth from your body, and I will establish his kingdom. He shall build a house for my name, and I will establish the throne of his kingdom forever. I will be a father to him, and he shall be a son to me. When he commits iniquity, I will punish him with a rod such as mortals use, with blows inflicted by human beings. But I will not take my steadfast love from him, as I took it from Saul, whom I put away from before you. Your house and your kingdom shall be made sure forever before me; your throne shall be established forever. In accordance with all these words and with all this vision, Nathan spoke to David.

## Passionate People

The church is filled with passionate people who mean well and want to accomplish great things for God. Religious zeal is no new thing. Wherever the faithful are gathered, regardless of their religion, there are some who want to charge headlong into a cause, a project, or a mission. It may be a function of personality, or training, that shapes people for religious zealotry. Don't get me wrong, I'm not saying zeal is inherently bad. Though it can cause a certain level of blindness as a zealot confidently charges onward.

Some might label King David a zealot. After all, you don't go headlong into battle against a giant with only a sling and some stones as weapons without being convinced of God's approval of your actions. There are other examples we could point to, as well. Regardless of King David's zeal, and despite some rather egregious mistakes, David earns the moniker, "man after God's heart." In today's passage, David's heart is pure, and his mind is clear.

God has given David rest from the enemies that surround his Kingdom. In his rest, David comes to realize that while he's living large in a palace, the ark of God still lives in a tent. David becomes convinced of the need to build God a temple, a permanent living space. Wisely, David consults with the prophet Nathan. You may remember Nathan from the Bathsheba incident. He delivered God's judgment on David, condemning the King's actions.

At first, Nathan tells his king that David can go ahead and build a temple for God. But later that night, God tells Nathan that David is not to go ahead with the building program. Instead, God will build a house out of David's descendants, one of which will construct a temple for Israel's God.

Nathan communicates God's verdict to David, and David listens and obeys. But what would have happened if David left his zeal for God to take over, clouding his judgment? Would David had gone ahead and started the building project? Would it have been a disaster? We'll never know because David was obedient.

How often do we allow our religious zeal to blind us from doing what God really wants us to do? How often do we charge ahead with a project or mission thinking, "Surely this is what God requires of us!" only to have it all fall apart? Or, maybe it's successful, but on our way to completing the project, we run roughshod over others, causing more harm than good. Do we allow ourselves to be consumed by what we think God wants so that we're unable to discern God's true calling?

Sadly, it happens more than we'd like to admit. You might be saying, "But David had Nathan who spoke directly to God! Where's our Nathan?" The answer is simple, your Nathan sits next to you during Sunday worship or across the table from you in a bible study. God's intention for the church is to be a place of communal discernment of the will of God. We're to work together in mutual submission and deference so that we might not be blinded by our well-intentioned zeal. It's a slow process, a process not conducive to rushing. It is a process bathed in prayer and scripture.

*Prayer: Oh God, help us to slow down and discern with our fellow believers the way that you would have us go. Help us to see your guidance in the loving words of our brothers and sisters in Christ. Amen.*

*Lectio Divina (Sacred Reading)*

**Galatians 4:1-7**

My point is this: heirs, as long as they are minors, are no better than slaves, though they are the owners of all the property; but they remain under guardians and trustees until the date set by the father. So with us; while we were minors, we were enslaved to the elemental spirits of the world. But when the fullness of time had come, God sent his Son, born of a woman, born under the law, in order to redeem those who were under the law, so that we might receive adoption as children. And because you are children, God has sent the Spirit of his Son into our hearts, crying, "Abba! Father!" So you are no longer a slave but a child, and if a child then also an heir, through God.

Formerly, when you did not know God, you were enslaved to beings that by nature are not gods. Now, however, that you have come to know God, or rather to be known by God, how can you turn back again to the weak and beggarly elemental spirits? How can you want to be enslaved to them again? You are observing special days, and months, and seasons, and years. I am afraid that my work for you may have been wasted.

Friends, I beg you, become as I am, for I also have become as you are. You have done me no wrong. You know that it was because of a physical infirmity that I first announced the gospel to you; though my condition put you to the test, you did not scorn or despise me, but welcomed me as an angel of God, as Christ Jesus. What has become of the goodwill you felt? For I testify that, had it been possible, you would have torn out your eyes and given them to me. Have I now become your enemy by telling you the truth? They make much of you, but for no good purpose; they want to exclude you, so that you may make much of them.

*Additional Texts: Psalm 80:1-7, 17-19; 2 Samuel 7:18-22*

**What If?**

In Advent's already-not-yet tension of celebrating the impending birth of Jesus and looking forward to Christ's coming again lies a gift: reminders of our identity. While David was coming to terms with a prophecy that his house and legacy would extend into the distant future, Paul was concerned that his congregation of Gentile converts would embrace that they were heirs of this same legacy through God's work in Jesus Christ.

Perhaps we can relate to the real-life experience of Christ followers in Galatia more than we know. They faced the pressures of a culture trying to pull them back into their pre-converted ways of living and thinking that they were the shapers of their own destiny. They faced the pull of other religious leaders who pressured them to follow a particular set of beliefs and practices rooted in Jewish law and ritual, namely circumcision, rules related to the Sabbath, festivals, and food prohibitions. Paul was concerned they would be enslaved by the pressures to conform.

When we face pressures to be this and to do that, it seems as though these external forces are chipping away at who we are at the very center of our being. After a while, we lose our grip on our values, mission, and identity. The pressures of consumerism in this season consistently pull us toward materialism. They not only become the chains that bind us but also lead us into debt in our efforts to chase unrealistic ideals. Like Paul, we can prepare the way by leaning into the Word, God's story, and reminding ourselves of our core identity so that this season of celebrating the birth of Jesus can become a season of new birth for us.

Paul counters the demands of culture and religion by rehearsing the story of who they have become through faith in Christ and their identity in God's Son. This very human son faced all the pressures we face from culture and religious law. Yet he came with a specific mission: liberate others in the same circumstance, adopting them into God's family with roots stretching back to David. At the moment of our adoption, God sent the Spirit into our hearts, grafted into our DNA. When we respond with cries of "Abba! Father!" we recognize somewhere deep down in our core that we belong. We are God's beloved. We are God's children. We are heirs whose inheritance is in the promise of Jesus the Christ. In this, we rejoice!

Our world aches for a sense of belonging. What if, Friends, in remembering who we are in this holy season, we also reconnect with our mission of sharing our adoption story so that others might be equally liberated? What if this Advent, we extend an invitation to others to join us in preparing the way for Jesus? What if, at the culmination of our shared journey, they, too, experience this holy adoption? What if they realize a truer sense of belonging? For this, we rejoice!

*Prayer: Oh God, thank you for adopting as your beloved children. Help us to share our story so that others might also enter into the joy of your adoption.*

*Lectio Divina (Sacred Reading)*

**John 3:22-36**

After this Jesus and his disciples went into the Judean countryside, and he spent some time there with them and baptized. John also was baptizing at Aenon near Salim because water was abundant there; and people kept coming and were being baptized — John, of course, had not yet been thrown into prison. Now a discussion about purification arose between John's disciples and a Jew. They came to John and said to him, "Rabbi, the one who was with you across the Jordan, to whom you testified, here he is baptizing, and all are going to him." John answered, "No one can receive anything except what has been given from heaven. You yourselves are my witnesses that I said, 'I am not the Messiah, but I have been sent ahead of him. 'He who has the bride is the bridegroom. The friend of the bridegroom, who stands and hears him, rejoices greatly at the bridegroom's voice. For this reason my joy has been fulfilled. He must increase, but I must decrease."

The one who comes from above is above all; the one who is of the earth belongs to the earth and speaks about earthly things. The one who comes from heaven is above all. He testifies to what he has seen and heard, yet no one accepts his testimony. Whoever has accepted his testimony has certified this, that God is true. He whom God has sent speaks the words of God, for he gives the Spirit without measure. The Father loves the Son and has placed all things in his hands. Whoever believes in the Son has eternal life; whoever disobeys the Son will not see life, but must endure God's wrath.

**Getting Smaller**

Pretty soon it will be that time of year when everyone wants to lose weight. Chances are, at one time you made a new year's resolution to drop a few pounds or to exercise more. So, you sign up for that weight loss plan or join the local gym. A friend who used to manage a gym once told me that most workout locations make the majority of their money in the month of January. Yes, we all want to be smaller. That is, in regard to body fat content. Guys want to be bigger, but not around the middle section, only in the arms and the chest. So, we beat our bodies, deprive our stomachs, all the while taking progress pictures in the bathroom or hallway mirror.

Of course, there's nothing wrong with wanting to be less fat. It's a good thing actually. It means that we're getting our priorities right. A healthy body honors God: it means we're taking care of this marvelous gift we've been given. John's gospel has introduced us to John the Baptist and to Jesus. Both are pretty important characters in the story and to the people of Israel. Both, it seems, have disciples. Both have been about the business of baptizing people.

John's disciples want to know his take on Jesus and the work he's doing. Though by their tone, they're a little jealous that Jesus is cutting into their market share of baptisms. John knows his place though, and it's not as master but as a servant, not the groom but the groomsman. It's not his day to celebrate for himself.

John shuts down the discussion with his disciples in verse 30 with this one little phrase, "he must increase, but I must decrease." John needs to get smaller, and he knows it.

The beginning of the year is a good time for us to get serious about our physical health, about the amount of fat we've got stored up, but about the size of our ego, too. Maybe it's the case that over the past year we've gotten a little too full of ourselves? Maybe we've gained a few pounds thinking we're more important than we really are? Maybe we've added a few inches around the waist because we believe that we don't need God to make things work out in our lives? Whatever the case may be, it's time for us to get smaller. It's time for us to decrease while Christ increases. It's time for us to have a proper understanding of our own standing in relationship to the one who created us in the first place. So, this year, resolve to lose some weight and to decrease in terms of your relationship with Christ. Allow Jesus 'influence in your life to increase. Let your ego become smaller and smaller so that you might be the person and do the work that God has called you to do!

*Prayer: Oh God, forgive us for being overly concerned with our own importance. Help us to decrease while you increase in importance in our lives. Amen.*

## The Examen
*Ask God for Illumination*

Speak to us O Lord.
Speak to us as wait and as we watch,
Speak to us as we hope and as we long,
As we sorrow, sigh, and rejoice.
Speak to us throughout these days of Advent
As we await the coming of Christ our King
And stay by us Lord we pray
Until you come again.

*Give Thanks*
- What can you give thanks for from this week?
- Remember the ways God has sustained and carried you this week

*Review the Week*
- Where have I seen God this week?
- Look at this past week through the eyes of God, rather than my own

*Name your Shortcomings*
- Reflect on those areas where you did not love God and neighbor as you should
- Reflect on those things left undone that should be done, and those things done that should not have been done

*Ask for forgiveness*
- Embrace this Upcoming Week
- Ask God where you need to be this week

# THE FOURTH WEEK OF ADVENT

*Collect*

Purify our conscience, Almighty God, by your daily visitation, that your Son Jesus Christ, at his coming, may find in us a mansion prepared for himself; who lives and reigns with you, in the unity of the Holy Spirit, one God, now and forever. Amen.

*Visio Divina* (**Sacred Vision**)

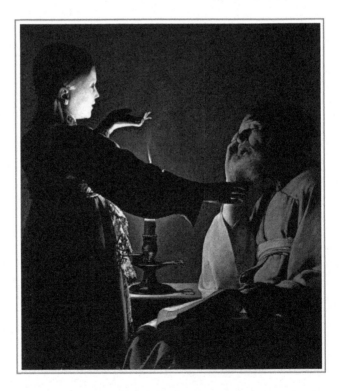

The Angel Visiting Joseph in a Dream
by Georges du Mesnil de La Tour

78

*Audio Divina* **(Sacred Listening)**
Songs for Worship
*O Come All Ye Faithful (His Name Shall Be)* - Passion Music Featuring Melodie Malone
*Joy to the World (Unspeakable Joy)* - Chris Tomlin
CCLI#2113365

Advent Reflection Playlist

*Prayer*
My Lord God, I have no idea where I am going. I do not see the road ahed of me. I cannot know for certain where it will end. Nor do I really know myself, and the fact that I think I am following Your will does not mean that I am actually doing so. But I believe that the desire to please You does in fact please you. And I hope I have that desire in all that I am doing. I hope that I will never do anything apart from that desire. And I know that, if I do this, You will lead me by the right road, though I may know nothing about it. Therefore, I will trust You always though I may seem to be lost and in the shadow of death. I will not fear, for You are ever with me, and You will never leave me to face my perils alone.
- Saint Thomas Merton

*Lectio Divina* **(Sacred Reading)**
Psalm 80:1-7, 17-19 - Qui regis Israel
Give ear, O Shepherd of Israel,
	you who lead Joseph like a flock!
	You who are enthroned upon the cherubim, shine forth
before Ephraim and Benjamin and Manasseh.
	Stir up your might,
		and come to save us!

Restore us, O God;

let your face shine, that we may be saved.

O Lord God of hosts,
   how long will you be angry with your people's prayers?
You have fed them with the bread of tears,
   and given them tears to drink in full measure.
You make us the scorn of our neighbors;
   our enemies laugh among themselves.

Restore us, O God of hosts;
   let your face shine, that we may be saved.

But let your hand be upon the one at your right hand,
   the one whom you made strong for yourself.
Then we will never turn back from you;
   give us life, and we will call on your name.

Restore us, O Lord God of hosts;
   let your face shine, that we may be saved.

### *Camino Divina* (Sacred Walking)

Sometime on Sunday, prayerfully light a candle to mark the beginning of your week. We light a candle and worship Jesus, the Light of the World, who was born to die so we might have true life and who is coming again in power and glory.

This week, you may wish to schedule a video call with friends or family over some coffee/tea/hot chocolate/eggnog and read the first two chapters of Luke out loud together. Take turns reading, or assign speaking parts to people, or have the kids stage a little skit. After reading it out loud together, discuss the magnitude of what these moments in the story of Jesus mean to you personally and to our world. As you read the Christmas stories, what do you learn about who God is and who we are as the people of God? Spend some time praying together, thanking God for coming to be with us in such an intimate way.

*Lectio Divina (Sacred Reading)*

**Genesis 17:15–22**

God said to Abraham, "As for Sarai your wife, you shall not call her Sarai, but Sarah shall be her name. I will bless her, and moreover I will give you a son by her. I will bless her, and she shall give rise to nations; kings of peoples shall come from her." Then Abraham fell on his face and laughed, and said to himself, "Can a child be born to a man who is a hundred years old? Can Sarah, who is ninety years old, bear a child?" And Abraham said to God, "O that Ishmael might live in your sight!" God said, "No, but your wife Sarah shall bear you a son, and you shall name him Isaac. I will establish my covenant with him as an everlasting covenant for his offspring after him. As for Ishmael, I have heard you; I will bless him and make him fruitful and exceedingly numerous; he shall be the father of twelve princes, and I will make him a great nation. But my covenant I will establish with Isaac, whom Sarah shall bear to you at this season next year." And when he had finished talking with him, God went up from Abraham.

*Additional Texts: 1 Samuel 2:1-10; Galatians 4:8-20*

**The Best Laid Plans**

Before our wedding day, my soon-to-be husband and I had the conversation: how many children shall we have? Although I am the eldest of two daughters, my mother was one of eight children. Our family gatherings were filled with good food, great conversations, laughter, and games. We knew our family had our back. While we envisioned my future husband's path as a college music professor, I envisioned myself as the occasional journalist, housewife, and mother of many. As we bartered over the number of children, I started high. "I'd like for us to have eight children," I said confidently, not in the least overwhelmed by the needs of a ten-member family. My fiancé nearly fell on the floor in laughter! "How about two," he countered through giggles. His laughter was contagious! I conceded to being a family of four.

Sometimes the best-laid plans don't come to fruition. Fast forward 29 years, and my partner and I are an ordained clergy couple who remain childless. Like countless others, we are familiar with the pain and, on occasion, the shame of infertility, the Biblical stories of infertile women resonate deep in my soul. My husband and I often joke that maybe we'll be like Abraham and Sarah starting our family after our first century of life. Considering we've both had relatives who've lived late into their ninth decade, it's not out of the realm of possibility. Yet it would take a supernatural act of God to make the prayers of our youth a reality. If God were to sidle up to my spouse today saying, "I'm going to bless your wife and also give you a child by her. I will bless her, and she shall give rise to nations," he would rejoice that I had been doubly blessed and then fall onto the ground in laughter like Abraham before him, just as he did at my suggestion of birthing a baseball team. Is it any wonder that God names the as-yet-unborn-son "Laughter?" Who says God doesn't have a sense of humor?

While some may argue that laughter is a sign of doubt, what if laughter is actually the first stage of belief? What if it's that first foothold of an idea, a hope, a dream? What if laughter creates space in our bodies, souls, and minds for a possible impossibility? If, in our anxiety and fear, our breathing becomes shallow, starving our brain of oxygen as well as the capacity to think outside the margins, what if laughter is restorative, giving our brains the oxygen and fuel it needs to step outside the box of what is into the realm of God's possible? If we plot the trajectory of God's covenant and the lineage of Jesus, today's reading enables us to extend the line from Abraham to Isaac. Yet I invite you, in this last week of preparation for the Advent of Jesus, to create space for laughter. Not only will your soul feel lighter, but you might also build your belief muscles.

*Prayer: Oh God, forgive us for our disbelief. As we try to imagine your grace-filled future for creation, may our laughter be a sign of our growing faith in you.*

*Lectio Divina (Sacred Reading)*

**2 Peter 1:12-22**

Therefore, I intend to keep on reminding you of these things, though you know them already and are established in the truth that has come to you. I think it right, as long as I am in this body, to refresh your memory, since I know that my death will come soon, as indeed our Lord Jesus Christ has made clear to me. And I will make every effort so that after my departure you may be able at any time to recall these things.

For we did not follow cleverly devised myths when we made known to you the power and coming of our Lord Jesus Christ, but we had been eyewitnesses of his majesty. For he received honor and glory from God the Father when that voice was conveyed to him by the Majestic Glory, saying, "This is my Son, my Beloved, with whom I am well pleased." We ourselves heard this voice come from heaven, while we were with him on the holy mountain.

So we have the prophetic message more fully confirmed. You will do well to be attentive to this as to a lamp shining in a dark place, until the day dawns and the morning star rises in your hearts. First of all you must understand this, that no prophecy of scripture is a matter of one's own interpretation, because no prophecy ever came by human will, but men and women moved by the Holy Spirit spoke from God.

**This is My Son, My Beloved**

It seems that it is human nature to forget. We forget all manner of things. We forget little things like taking out the trash or starting the dishwasher. In fact, an entire portion of the technology industry is dedicated to helping us remember things. Of course, I'm not just talking about the little day-to-day type of things; I mean, sometimes we forget the really big things, like who we are or who we should be.

83

As we get to verse 12 of this first chapter in Peter's second letter, we are told that his main concern is to constantly remind us of how God has already given us what we need but that we need to work to truly understand and utilize those gifts. Peter wants to continue to remind us of those things because they are of the utmost importance. Peter's life draws to a close, and well, he wants us to remain steadfast in the faith after he's gone.

What a gift Peter has given us, the gift of a faith well remembered! This should be our aspiration, too, to live so deeply in our faith, constantly reminding those that come after us of the gifts we have received. Will your children, will the children of your church, remember their faith after you are gone?

As Peter moves on, we find that what is important to Peter is not a cleverly devised production or a brilliant delivery but the simple truth of the power and coming of Christ, which he witnessed as he heard the voice of God declaring, "This is my Son, my Beloved, which whom I am well pleased."

As we wait for the return of this Beloved Son, let us do so in an active manner. Let us remind ourselves and those who follow us of these great gifts we have received. Let us remind ourselves of the message that God himself became one of us so that we might become like him.

Indeed, over the years, many have given into humanity's tendency to forget. They have forgotten the trash and the dishwasher, but they have also forgotten the gifts they have received and the giver of those gifts. Let us not become like them!

*Prayer: Oh God, help us to remember the good gifts you have given us - the gifts of love, and life, and salvation. Help us to help those who come after to remember those things, too. Amen.*

*Lectio Divina (Sacred Reading)*

**Matthew 1:1-17**

An account of the genealogy of Jesus the Messiah, the son of David, the son of Abraham.

Abraham was the father of Isaac, and Isaac the father of Jacob, and Jacob the father of Judah and his brothers, and Judah the father of Perez and Zerah by Tamar, and Perez the father of Hezron, and Hezron the father of Aram, and Aram the father of Aminadab, and Aminadab the father of Nahshon, and Nahshon the father of Salmon, and Salmon the father of Boaz by Rahab, and Boaz the father of Obed by Ruth, and Obed the father of Jesse, and Jesse the father of King David.

And David was the father of Solomon by the wife of Uriah, and Solomon the father of Rehoboam, and Rehoboam the father of Abijah, and Abijah the father of Asaph, and Asaph the father of Jehoshaphat, and Jehoshaphat the father of Joram, and Joram the father of Uzziah, and Uzziah the father of Jotham, and Jotham the father of Ahaz, and Ahaz the father of Hezekiah, and Hezekiah the father of Manasseh, and Manasseh the father of Amos, and Amos the father of Josiah, and Josiah the father of Jechoniah and his brothers, at the time of the deportation to Babylon.

And after the deportation to Babylon: Jechoniah was the father of Salathiel, and Salathiel the father of Zerubbabel, and Zerubbabel the father of Abiud, and Abiud the father of Eliakim, and Eliakim the father of Azor, and Azor the father of Zadok, and Zadok the father of Achim, and Achim the father of Eliud, and Eliud the father of Eleazar, and Eleazar the father of Matthan, and Matthan the father of Jacob, and Jacob the father of Joseph the husband of Mary, of whom Jesus was born, who is called the Messiah.

So all the generations from Abraham to David are fourteen generations; and from David to the deportation to Babylon, fourteen generations; and from the deportation to Babylon to the Messiah, fourteen generations.

*Additional Texts: 1 Samuel 2:1-10; Genesis 37:2-11*

### Roots

Within the last year, I have been bitten by the genealogy bug. I credit the work of Henry Louis Gates, Jr. and his PBS show Finding Your Roots. As he and his team trace the lineage of his guests, he weaves an intimate and revealing family history. Interestingly, each guest has a particular reason for embarking on the search, sometimes a family mystery and other times stories that remain untold. Yet each guest comes away with a deeper understanding of the ways in which life experiences and historical events have impacted their ancestors, shaping who they are today.

Clearly, Jesus did not sit across a table from Matthew with a family mystery to be solved. It's not a genealogy the Son of God requested. Commentaries point out that neither the genealogy nor the math of the generations is very accurate. There are several inconsistencies between the genealogies of Matthew and Luke. And so, as I stumble over my pronunciation of some of the names, I wonder: Why start the Good News with a genealogy? Why include these particular ancestors? What was Matthew's goal?

It is helpful to know that Matthew's church, the only gospel writer to use the Greek word for church to describe his faith community, was surrounded by a strong, both in practice and number, Jewish population. While there may have been Gentile converts in his community, a majority would have been steeped in scripture as well as Jewish rituals and festivals. Matthew's genealogy doesn't serve as a birth announcement. Rather he is intentionally connecting the covenant and promise carved in the Hebrew Bible with Jesus, the fulfillment of that Messianic hope. He intentionally connects Jesus with Abraham, through whom God initiated the covenant, tracing a lineage through those ancestors who continued to carry the covenant all the way up to the line of Kings. Then the writer intentionally links Jesus with David to highlight Jesus 'kingship of a kingdom that is not of this earth. Matthew even dares to list five women, four by name, one by marital relationship, so that not just the messianic community but, more so, Jesus 'kingdom is inclusive of women and men of all ethnicities, creeds, classes, and customs. The naming of women in the genealogy reminds Matthew's community that God will surprise us; God will step outside the box and draw into the covenant the people we least expect to be worthy of inclusion. These are the roots of God's Beloved Kingdom.

Ultimately, Matthew considered his message and his audience. He considered what those outside the church needed to hear, know, and trust to believe. Jesus ' genealogy prepares the way to faith in the Great Redeemer, Jesus the Messiah, the son of David, the son of Abraham. If the message is so important that Matthew would craft an introduction to his gospel designed to lead people to the truth, how much more will God do to prepare the way toward belief for us and those who don't even know Jesus yet? This is the blessing of prevenient grace that always goes before us, preparing the way, even in this holy season of expectation and the advent of new life.

*Prayer: Oh God, thank you for the abundant grace that draws us to you. Thank you for preparing the way for us to believe. In your grace, help us to prepare the way for others to believe as well.*

*Lectio Divina (Sacred Reading)*

**John 14:1-17**

"Do not let your hearts be troubled. Believe in God, believe also in me. In my Father's house there are many dwelling places. If it were not so, would I have told you that I go to prepare a place for you?And if I go and prepare a place for you, I will come again and will take you to myself, so that where I am, there you may be also. And you know the way to the place where I am going."Thomas said to him, "Lord, we do not know where you are going. How can we know the way?" Jesus said to him, "I am the way, and the truth, and the life. No one comes to the Father except through me. If you know me, you will know my Father also. From now on you do know him and have seen him."

Philip said to him, "Lord, show us the Father, and we will be satisfied." Jesus said to him, "Have I been with you all this time, Philip, and you still do not know me? Whoever has seen me has seen the Father. How can you say, 'Show us the Father'? Do you not believe that I am in the Father and the Father is in me? The words that I say to you I do not speak on my own; but the Father who dwells in me does his works. Believe me that I am in the Father and the Father is in me; but if you do not, then believe me because of the works themselves. Very truly, I tell you, the one who believes in me will also do the works that I do and, in fact, will do greater works than these, because I am going to the Father. I will do whatever you ask in my name, so that the Father may be glorified in the Son. If in my name you ask me for anything, I will do it.

"If you love me, you will keep my commandments. And I will ask the Father, and he will give you another Advocate, to be with you forever. This is the Spirit of truth, whom the world cannot receive, because it neither sees him nor knows him. You know him, because he abides with you, and he will be in you.

**Good Drivers**

Have you ever had to follow someone in a car? Before the days of GPS built into every phone, if you were going somewhere in a group and you didn't know how to get there, the best way was to follow someone in another car who did know the way. We did this a lot when I was in High School. As a group of friends, we would head over to someone's house after work or church and inevitably someone would not know the way.

Now, not all drivers are good at being the lead car. They either drive too fast, aren't aware of how many cars are following them, or they pull out into traffic where there is only enough space for one car to safely merge. On the other hand, some drivers are particularly adept at showing the way. They know exactly how many cars are behind them. They drive right at the speed limit or a little below, knowing that the trail car will have to speed significantly if they want to catch up. Good lead car drivers know if everyone will make it through a green light or not, and if for some reason they don't all make it, they will slow down or pull over until everyone has caught up. Driving the lead car is really a form of art.

Jesus is a superb lead driver, although the disciples aren't quite sure about that. If we're honest, we may not be either. Jesus tries to reassure his disciples about where he is leading them. He wants them to know that even though he is going away, he's going to prepare a place for them. He's also trying to assure them that they already know the way. Thomas protests, "Lord, we do not know where you are going." Thomas 'words are familiar to us all. If we've not said them verbally, we've thought it. "God, what in the world are you doing? You're leading me somewhere, right?"

In verse 7, Jesus utters words that should be the end of the discussion. "If you know me, you will know my Father also. From now on, you do know him and have seen him." So often we don't trust where Jesus is taking us because we don't believe that he's leading us in the right direction. Over and over again, Jesus tries to reassure us that he's really and truly one with the Father! He's God! He knows where we're all headed. We just need to follow.

As we head toward Christmas, let us trust that this baby that is to be born truly is God and trust that he really is a good lead driver.

*Prayer: Oh God, help us to truly follow Jesus. Help us to focus on Jesus and not question the direction he leads us. Amen.*

*Lectio Divina (Sacred Reading)*

**2 Samuel 7:18, 23-29**

Then King David went in and sat before the Lord, and said, "Who am I, O Lord God, and what is my house, that you have brought me thus far?

Who is like your people, like Israel? Is there another nation on earth whose God went to redeem it as a people, and to make a name for himself, doing great and awesome things for them, by driving out before his people nations and their gods? And you established your people Israel for yourself to be your people forever; and you, O Lord, became their God. And now, O Lord God, as for the word that you have spoken concerning your servant and concerning his house, confirm it forever; do as you have promised. Thus your name will be magnified forever in the saying, 'The Lord of hosts is God over Israel'; and the house of your servant David will be established before you. For you, O Lord of hosts, the God of Israel, have made this revelation to your servant, saying, 'I will build you a house'; therefore your servant has found courage to pray this prayer to you. And now, O Lord God, you are God, and your words are true, and you have promised this good thing to your servant; now therefore may it please you to bless the house of your servant, so that it may continue forever before you; for you, O Lord God, have spoken, and with your blessing shall the house of your servant be blessed forever."

*Additional Texts: Luke 1:46b-55; Galatians 3:6-14*

**No Expiration Date**

It's been said that the prayers we pray for others never expire. The implication is that the prayers our ancestors lifted on our behalf are timeless. These ancient prayers are as alive for us today as they were born in the hearts, shaped in the minds, and uttered from the lips of those who loved us even before they knew us.

91

Without a doubt, King David was a gifted leader. Yet it was his relationship with God that gave him life and hope. In one breath, he could praise God for God's mighty deeds, point out the motivation for the LORD'S actions, and in the next breath pivot to a prayer of petition rooted in a promise: "For you, O LORD of hosts, the God of Israel, have made this revelation to your servant, saying, 'I will build you a house; 'therefore your servant has found courage to pray this prayer to you" (2 Samuel 7: 27, NRSVUE). While celebrating God's covenant and blessing he already experiences on his own house, David asks that the promise, the blessing, and this very house will go on forever. He vocalizes a timeless prayer with eternal consequences beyond his imagination. David could not visualize that God's reply to his prayer would be enfleshed. Nor could he imagine that there would be room enough in his forever house for the whole world.

Mary, too, was the recipient of a life-changing revelation: she would birth the promise made "to Abraham and to his descendants forever" (Luke 1:55, NRSVUE), a promise robed in flesh, a promise intoned in the prayers of King David for a forever blessing upon his house. Her song of praise is more than a catalog of the character and work of the Mighty One throughout history. It betrays a confidence that the Mighty One will keep on doing these same things through the One she carries in her own body. St. Augustine has said that when we sing, we pray twice. In which case, Mary's song is her hope-laden prayer born in her heart, shaped in her mind, given voice through the lips of one who loved her son before she knew him—a Son whose love would encompass the whole world.

*Prayer: Oh God, grant us the vision to see the possibilities of your promises. Amen.*

*Lectio Divina (Sacred Reading)*

**Zechariah 2:1-13**

I looked up and saw a man with a measuring line in his hand. Then I asked, "Where are you going?" He answered me, "To measure Jerusalem, to see what is its width and what is its length." Then the angel who talked with me came forward, and another angel came forward to meet him, and said to him, "Run, say to that young man: Jerusalem shall be inhabited like villages without walls, because of the multitude of people and animals in it. For I will be a wall of fire all around it, says the Lord, and I will be the glory within it."

Up, up! Flee from the land of the north, says the Lord; for I have spread you abroad like the four winds of heaven, says the Lord. Up! Escape to Zion, you that live with daughter Babylon. For thus said the Lord of hosts (after his glory sent me) regarding the nations that plundered you: Truly, one who touches you touches the apple of my eye. See now, I am going to raise my hand against them, and they shall become plunder for their own slaves. Then you will know that the Lord of hosts has sent me. Sing and rejoice, O daughter Zion! For lo, I will come and dwell in your midst, says the Lord. Many nations shall join themselves to the Lord on that day, and shall be my people; and I will dwell in your midst. And you shall know that the Lord of hosts has sent me to you. The Lord will inherit Judah as his portion in the holy land, and will again choose Jerusalem.

Be silent, all people, before the Lord; for he has roused himself from his holy dwelling.

**Words of Joy**

Earlier in our Advent readings, we've encountered the harsh reality that accompanies the coming of God. Like Matthew's gospel, the book of Amos makes it very clear that the coming of God is a time of dread. God's coming always brings judgment on those who aren't fully prepared, and preparedness always has to do with a full obedience to God's will.

As we begin to turn the corner toward Christmas Day, the coming of God becomes a more joyful event. For Israel at least, God's coming leads them off into the judgment of exile. God's second coming leads them home. For Zechariah, the ugly realities of exile are drawing to a close. He's having visions of his people returning to the land they once called home. Zechariah meets a messenger from God who is measuring the perimeter of Jerusalem. He's seeing if it's big enough to hold all of the inhabitants who will now dwell in a renewed Jerusalem.

In an interlude between his third and fourth visions, Zechariah begins to encourage the people to sing and rejoice because God is coming again. This time, God is not coming in judgment but with reconciliation and restoration. God is coming, not to condemn but to dwell in the midst of the people. While these words would have been powerful for those in exile in Babylon, they have not lost their power for us today. We too sit in the darkness of exile, but we hear Zechariah's words as words of joy because God is coming, not to destroy the world but to establish his residence in our midst.

We must never skip over the tough parts of the Bible, which pronounce terrible things like judgment and exile. We must not skip those parts because they always encourage us to live lives of complete obedience and faithfulness to the Father. Yet, we must always read those parts of the Bible with one eye toward the future, with one eye fixed on passages like this one in Zechariah. Judgement without hope is useless. Our hope is a faith-filled hope.

In the middle of woe and weal, in the middle of hardship, that of our own making and that of which has been showered on us by others, we must always remember that God is coming again to free us from those things. God is coming to bring us home, to situate himself in our midsts.

As you move off into your day today, remember that Christ is coming to live among us as one of us. His purpose is to bring us home from exile. His mission is to undo all of the hurt and pain in our world. Have faith. Have hope. Rejoice because our God is coming.

*Prayer: Oh God, help us to wait patiently for your coming. Help us not lose hope that you're coming again to make the world right. Amen.*

**The Examen**

*Ask God for Illumination*

Speak to us O Lord.
Speak to us as wait and as we watch,
Speak to us as we hope and as we long,
As we sorrow, sigh, and rejoice.
Speak to us throughout these days of Advent
As we await the coming of Christ our King
And stay by us Lord we pray
Until you come again.

*Give Thanks*
- What can you give thanks for from this week?
- Remember the ways God has sustained and carried you this week

*Review the Week*
- Where have I seen God this week?
- Look at this past week through the eyes of God, rather than my own

*Name your Shortcomings*
- Reflect on those areas where you did not love God and neighbor as you should
- Reflect on those things left undone that should be done, and those things done that should not have been done

*Ask for forgiveness*
- Embrace this Upcoming Week
- Ask God where you need to be this week

### Station 1: The Annunciation

We adore you O Christ and praise you for you for by your holy birth you become one of us in order to redeem and save.

**Luke 1:26-38**
In the sixth month the angel Gabriel was sent by God to a town in Galilee called Nazareth, to a virgin engaged to a man whose name was Joseph, of the house of David. The virgin's name was Mary. And he came to her and said, "Greetings, favored one! The Lord is with you." But she was much perplexed by his words and pondered what sort of greeting this might be. The angel said to her, "Do not be afraid, Mary, for you have found favor with God. And now, you will conceive in your womb and bear a son, and you will name him Jesus. He will be

96

great and will be called the Son of the Most High, and the Lord God will give to him the throne of his ancestor David. He will reign over the house of Jacob forever, and of his kingdom there will be no end." Mary said to the angel, "How can this be, since I am a virgin?" The angel said to her, "The Holy Spirit will come upon you, and the power of the Most High will overshadow you; therefore the child to be born will be holy; he will be called Son of God. And now, your relative Elizabeth in her old age has also conceived a son, and this is the sixth month for her who was said to be barren. For nothing will be impossible with God." Then Mary said, "Here am I, the servant of the Lord; let it be with me according to your word." Then the angel departed from her.

The Word became flesh and dwelt among us.
We have seen his glory, the glory of the only Son from the Father, full of grace and truth.

## Station 2: The Visitation

We adore you O Christ and praise you for you for by your holy birth you become one of us in order to redeem and save.

### Luke 1:39-45

In those days Mary set out and went with haste to a Judean town in the hill country, where she entered the house of Zechariah and greeted Elizabeth. When Elizabeth heard Mary's greeting, the child leaped in her womb. And Elizabeth was filled with the Holy Spirit and exclaimed with a loud cry, "Blessed are you among women, and blessed is the fruit of your womb. And why has this happened to me, that the mother of my Lord comes to me? For as soon as I heard the sound of your greeting, the child in my womb leaped for joy. And blessed is she who believed that there would be a fulfillment of what was spoken to her by the Lord."

The Word became flesh and dwelt among us.
We have seen his glory, the glory of the only Son from the Father, full of grace and truth.

## Station 3: The Magnificat

We adore you O Christ and praise you for you for by your holy birth you become one of us in order to redeem and save.

**Luke 1:46-55**

And Mary said,

"My soul magnifies the Lord,

and my spirit rejoices in God my Savior,
for he has looked with favor on the lowly state of his servant.

Surely from now on all generations will call me blessed,

for the Mighty One has done great things for me,
    and holy is his name;
indeed, his mercy is for those who fear him
    from generation to generation.
He has shown strength with his arm;
    he has scattered the proud in the imagination of their hearts.
He has brought down the powerful from their thrones
    and lifted up the lowly;
he has filled the hungry with good things
    and sent the rich away empty.
He has come to the aid of his child Israel,
    in remembrance of his mercy,
according to the promise he made to our ancestors,
    to Abraham and to his descendants forever."

The Word became flesh and dwelt among us.
We have seen his glory, the glory of the only Son from the Father, full of grace and truth.

## Station 4: The Dream of Joseph

We adore you O Christ and praise you for you for by your holy birth you become one of us in order to redeem and save.

**Matthew 1:18-25**
Now the birth of Jesus the Messiah took place in this way. When his mother Mary had been engaged to Joseph, but before they lived together, she was found to be pregnant from the Holy Spirit. Her husband Joseph, being a righteous man and unwilling to expose her to public disgrace, planned to divorce her quietly. But just when he had resolved to do this, an angel of the Lord appeared to him in a dream and said, "Joseph, son of David, do not be afraid to take Mary as your wife, for the child conceived in her is from the Holy Spirit. She will bear a son, and you are to name him Jesus, for he will save his people from their sins." All this took place to fulfill what had been spoken by the Lord through the prophet:

"Look, the virgin shall become pregnant and give birth to a son,

and they shall name him Emmanuel,"which means, "God is with us."

When Joseph awoke from sleep, he did as the angel of the Lord commanded him; he took her as his wife but had no marital relations with her until she had given birth to a son, and he named him Jesus.

The Word became flesh and dwelt among us.
We have seen his glory, the glory of the only Son from the Father, full of grace and truth.

We adore you O Christ and praise you for you for by your holy birth you become one of us in order to redeem and save.

**Luke 2:1-5**
In those days a decree went out from Caesar Augustus that all the world should be registered. This was the first registration and was taken while Quirinius was governor of Syria. All went to their own towns to be registered. Joseph also went from the town of Nazareth in Galilee to Judea, to the city of David called Bethlehem, because he was descended from the house and family of David. He

went to be registered with Mary, to whom he was engaged and who was expecting a child.

The Word became flesh and dwelt among us.
We have seen his glory, the glory of the only Son from the Father, full of grace and truth.

## Station 6: The Birth of Jesus

We adore you O Christ and praise you for you for by your holy birth you become one of us in order to redeem and save.

**Luke 2:6-7**
While they were there, the time came for her to deliver her child. And she gave birth to her firstborn son and wrapped him in bands of cloth and laid him in a manger, because there was no place in the guest room.

The Word became flesh and dwelt among us.
We have seen his glory, the glory of the only Son from the Father, full of grace and truth.

## Station 7: The Announcement of the Angels

We adore you O Christ and praise you for you for by your holy birth you become one of us in order to redeem and save.

**Luke 2:8-14**
Now in that same region there were shepherds living in the fields, keeping watch over their flock by night. Then an angel of the Lord stood before them, and the glory of the Lord shone around them, and they were terrified. But the angel said to them, "Do not be afraid, for see, I am bringing you good news of great joy for all the people: to you is born this day in the city of David a Savior, who is the Messiah, the Lord. This will be a sign for you: you will find a child wrapped in bands of cloth and lying in a manger." And suddenly there was with the angel a multitude of the heavenly host, praising God and saying,

"Glory to God in the highest heaven,
    and on earth peace among those whom he favors!"

The Word became flesh and dwelt among us.
We have seen his glory, the glory of the only Son from the Father, full of grace and truth.

## Station 8: The Shepherds come to the Manger

We adore you O Christ and praise you for you for by your holy birth you become one of us in order to redeem and save.

**Luke 2:15-20**

When the angels had left them and gone into heaven, the shepherds said to one another, "Let us go now to Bethlehem and see this thing that has taken place, which the Lord has made known to us." So they went with haste and found Mary and Joseph and the child lying in the manger. When they saw this, they made known what had been told them about this child, and all who heard it were amazed at what the shepherds told them, and Mary treasured all these words and pondered them in her heart. The shepherds returned, glorifying and praising God for all they had heard and seen, just as it had been told them.

The Word became flesh and dwelt among us.
We have seen his glory, the glory of the only Son from the Father, full of grace and truth.

**Station 9: The Holy Name of Jesus**

We adore you O Christ and praise you for you for by your holy birth you become one of us in order to redeem and save.

**Luke 2:21**
When the eighth day came, it was time to circumcise the child, and he was called Jesus, the name given by the angel before he was conceived in the womb.

The Word became flesh and dwelt among us.
We have seen his glory, the glory of the only Son from the Father, full of grace and truth.

## Station 10: The Presentation of Jesus in the Temple

We adore you O Christ and praise you for you for by your holy birth you become one of us in order to redeem and save.

**Luke 2:22-32**
When the time came for their purification according to the law of Moses, they brought him up to Jerusalem to present him to the Lord (as it is written in the law of the Lord, "Every firstborn male shall be designated as holy to the Lord"), and they offered a sacrifice according to what is stated in the law of the Lord, "a pair of turtledoves or two young pigeons."

Now there was a man in Jerusalem whose name was Simeon; this man was righteous and devout, looking forward to the consolation of Israel, and the Holy Spirit rested on him. It had been revealed to him by the Holy Spirit that he would not see death before he had seen the Lord's Messiah. Guided by the Spirit, Simeon came into the temple, and when the parents brought in the child Jesus to do for him what was customary under the law, Simeon took him in his arms and praised God, saying,

"Master, now you are dismissing your servant in peace,
  according to your word,
for my eyes have seen your salvation,
  which you have prepared in the presence of all peoples,
a light for revelation to the gentiles
  and for glory to your people Israel."

The Word became flesh and dwelt among us.
We have seen his glory, the glory of the only Son from the Father, full of grace and truth.

## Station 11: The Visit of the Magi

We adore you O Christ and praise you for you for by your holy birth you become one of us in order to redeem and save.

**Matthew 2:1-12**

In the time of King Herod, after Jesus was born in Bethlehem of Judea, magi from the east came to Jerusalem, asking, "Where is the child who has been born king of the Jews? For we observed his star in the east and have come to pay him homage." When King Herod heard this, he was frightened, and all Jerusalem with him, and calling together all the chief priests and scribes of the people, he inquired of them where the Messiah was to be born. They told him, "In Bethlehem of Judea, for so it has been written by the prophet:

'And you, Bethlehem, in the land of Judah,
    are by no means least among the rulers of Judah,
for from you shall come a ruler
    who is to shepherd my people Israel.'"

Then Herod secretly called for the magi and learned from them the exact time when the star had appeared. Then he sent them to Bethlehem, saying, "Go and search diligently for the child, and when you have found him, bring me word so that I may also go and pay him homage." When they had heard the king, they set out, and there, ahead of them, went the star that they had seen in the east, until it stopped over the place where the child was. When they saw that the star had stopped, they were overwhelmed with joy. On entering the house, they saw the child with Mary his mother, and they knelt down and paid him homage. Then, opening their treasure chests, they offered him gifts of gold, frankincense, and myrrh. And having been warned in a dream not to return to Herod, they left for their own country by another road.

The Word became flesh and dwelt among us.
We have seen his glory, the glory of the only Son from the Father, full of grace and truth.

## Station 12: The Flight to Egypt

We adore you O Christ and praise you for you for by your holy birth you become one of us in order to redeem and save.

**Matthew 2:13-15**
Now after they had left, an angel of the Lord appeared to Joseph in a dream and said, "Get up, take the child and his mother, and flee to Egypt, and remain there until I tell you, for Herod is about to search for the child, to destroy him." Then Joseph got up, took the child and his mother by night, and went to Egypt and remained there until the death of Herod. This was to fulfill what had been spoken by the Lord through the prophet, "Out of Egypt I have called my son."

The Word became flesh and dwelt among us.
We have seen his glory, the glory of the only Son from the Father, full of grace and truth.

## Station 13: The Death of the Innocents

We adore you O Christ and praise you for you for by your holy birth you become one of us in order to redeem and save.

**Matthew 2:16-18**
When Herod saw that he had been tricked by the magi, he was infuriated, and he sent and killed all the children in and around Bethlehem who were two years old or under, according to the time that he had learned from the magi. Then what had been spoken through the prophet Jeremiah was fulfilled:

"A voice was heard in Ramah,
 wailing and loud lamentation,
Rachel weeping for her children;
 she refused to be consoled, because they are no more."

115

The Word became flesh and dwelt among us.
We have seen his glory, the glory of the only Son from the Father, full of grace and truth.

## Station 14: The Return to Nazareth

We adore you O Christ and praise you for you for by your holy birth you become one of us in order to redeem and save.

**Matthew 2:19-23**

When Herod died, an angel of the Lord suddenly appeared in a dream to Joseph in Egypt and said, "Get up, take the child and his mother, and go to the land of Israel, for those who were seeking the child's life are dead." Then Joseph got up, took the child and his mother, and went to the land of Israel. But when he heard that Archelaus was ruling Judea in place of his father Herod, he was afraid to go there. And after being warned in a dream, he went away to the district of Galilee. There he made his home in a town called Nazareth, so that what had been spoken through the prophets might be fulfilled, "He will be called a Nazarene."

The Word became flesh and dwelt among us.
We have seen his glory, the glory of the only Son from the Father, full of grace and truth.

*All art is by James Tissort, except station 9 which is by Guido Reni.

Made in the USA
Coppell, TX
18 November 2022